EVERYGIRL'S
LIFEGUIDE

Dr. Miriam Stoppard
EVERYGIRL'S LIFEGUIDE

HEALTHCARE

DORLING KINDERSLEY
London • New York • Sydney • Moscow

Visit us on the World Wide Web at www.dk.com

A DORLING KINDERSLEY BOOK
Visit us on the World Wide Web at www.dk.com

DESIGN AND EDITORIAL   Edward Kinsey and
Jacqueline Jackson

SENIOR MANAGING ART
EDITOR   Lynne Brown
SENIOR MANAGING
EDITOR   Corinne Roberts

SENIOR ART EDITOR   Karen Ward
SENIOR EDITOR   Penny Warren

PRODUCTION   Sarah Coltman

First published by Dorling Kindersley in 1987

This edition published in 1999 by
Dorling Kindersley Limited, 9 Henrietta Street,
Covent Garden, London WC2E 8PS

A CIP catalogue record for this book is available
from the British Library

ISBN 0-7513-0619-3

Reproduced by Colourscan, Singapore
Printed in Hong Kong by Wing King Tong

CONTENTS

INTRODUCTION

During your early teenage years you'll find that, in addition to your physical shape, your personality and the way you behave will change quite dramatically. Part of this is due to an awareness of your own sexuality, which is caused by the start of your monthly periods and physical changes in your body, and part is due to an increase in certain hormones (chemicals produced by your ovaries) that have an effect on your moods. By the time you're about 18 or 19, you'll have reached your correct adult height and shape.

PHYSICAL AND EMOTIONAL CHANGES

The beginning of regular periods, usually about 18 months after your first period appears, means that you're capable of having a baby. This is a very dramatic sign that, physically at least, you're not a child any more. Yet in most other ways you're still treated as a child and you may regard yourself as a child, so it's no wonder you feel confused.

Your hormones can have an uneven effect on you. At one moment you'll feel quite happy, but soon afterwards quite unhappy. These "swinging" moods may also make you feel nervous, shy and anxious about yourself, so that you may want to be the same as and have the approval of others of your own age. You might find that you want to be alone more and more, and take to sitting in your room reading or listening to music. You may be short-tempered and it's possible that you'll have arguments with both your teachers and parents over things that are really quite unimportant. You may feel that the world is against you, and that you're being treated unfairly. You probably feel that no-one understands you or is capable of understanding you.

Most teenagers develop very high ideals and are concerned to do the best they can when they grow up. Because of this, many teenagers set themselves goals and aims that are far too high. If they cannot achieve them, they may then become unhappy with their performance and unhappy about themselves.

A number of girls feel that they lack control over their bodies. From time to time they also feel out of tune with their families, school mates, friends and especially their boyfriends. Very commonly, girls see themselves as second-rate and unattractive. In a survey that I did of teenagers' attitudes towards themselves I got responses like this, "I think I look terrible! My clothes are wrong, my make-up's wrong, my hair's wrong. Nothing's right. I'd like to be prettier and older."

Accepting yourself for what you are, warts and all, isn't easy but, if you expect too much of yourself, you may never feel that you're an "OK" person. It may be painful to realize that you may never be an award-winning novelist, a great painter, a powerful journalist, the greatest actress who ever lived or the most beautiful model. Very few of us achieve great fame, so it's best to be realistic and to strive for something that is within your capabilities. By setting your sights a little lower and maybe settling for a little less, you're more likely to succeed.

You're not alone if you feel afraid of the unknown. We're all scared of things we don't understand. The inevitable outcome of ignorance is anxiety. So one of the best ways to boost your confidence and help you to accept yourself as you are is to acquire more knowledge about growing up.

GETTING HELP

To my mind, the impersonal surroundings and atmosphere of the biology class are not ideal for learning about sex and relationships; these issues should be discussed in the supportive comfort of your home. Parents have a responsibility to help their teenagers grow up, and to provide the best kind of sex education. It's much better to hear about sex from your own parents, than to hear highly embellished and inaccurate stories from school mates. If you can't speak to your parents about sex, however, get help from elsewhere, but be sure to choose a reliable source. It's essential that you get dependable information and advice to help you with this issue. A teacher with whom you have a good relationship may be the one to turn to or a sympathetic relative who will listen and advise. Alternatively, you could approach a family doctor to whom you feel you can talk. A sensible friend of your own age, who would happily share information and problems, will certainly make you feel better, or you may know an older girl who has come through her teenage years and is able to see them simply as part of growing up. Their practical advice and healthy reassurance may change the way you see things, so that you're able to look at your problems calmly.

In my survey of teenagers' attitudes, a disappointingly high number of teenagers said that their parents were no help at all with problems about growing up. In fact, teenagers chose to speak to their parents last about many matters, and then only if they had to. However, you do need your parents because it's difficult to cope without them and their support, and you're unlikely to find anyone else who's as interested in you as they are. What's essential is to persuade them that you have important things to talk about while you're growing up and you need their help. Few parents can resist such a request. Given the chance, the majority of parents would rather their children came to them than go to another person.

EMERGING AS AN ADULT

Things are never done by halves in the teenage years. It's a time for putting 100 percent into everything you think and do. You are full of energy and find your life filling up with new interests and new friendships. Your teens are a very precious part of your life; your horizons broaden in a unique way and new choices constantly present themselves. This time is also unique because of how much you grow mentally. You enter the teenage years feeling awkward, clumsy, shy and bewildered and you emerge from them with clear opinions and ideas about your career, the kind of relationships that you're looking for and possibly the sort of life that's going to make you happy. Probably at no other time in your life will you grow at such a fast rate, both emotionally and intellectually.

There are few periods in our lives that seem as difficult as our teenage years, and when they're over, you'll probably look back and feel that you did very well in negotiating them. If you manage this, your achievement will be enormous. If you come to the end of this time feeling fairly contented with a positive outlook on life, it's a triumph.

1

PUBERTY

Between the ages of about 10 and 16, your body is transformed. Your breasts and hips become rounded, you develop pubic and underarm hair and, at around the age of 11 to 15, you start to have periods. These changes are usually troublefree, but some girls find that their periods are painful or irregular to begin with, and some may feel moody and get spots just before and during their periods. The more you understand what's happening to your body, the more straightforward puberty will be, so in this chapter I explain in detail the physical and mental changes you'll experience and give advice on choosing pads and tampons, as well as on dealing with menstrual problems.

HOW YOUR BODY CHANGES

Anatomically, girls are distinguished from boys by their primary sexual organs and secondary sexual characteristics. Your primary sexual organs are your ovaries, Fallopian tubes, uterus, cervix and vagina – in other words, everything to do with producing babies. The clitoris can also be considered part of this group.

The ovaries contain all the eggs (ova) necessary for you to make babies, and they also produce the female hormones oestrogen and progesterone, which as well as controlling the menstrual cycle, are responsible for your secondary sexual characteristics (see opposite).

The Fallopian tubes lead from the ovaries to the uterus, which is a hollow, pear-shaped organ in which a fertilized egg will develop into a baby. The vagina, which is about 8cm (3in) long, has extremely elastic walls that can stretch during intercourse and childbirth. The opening from the vagina into the uterus is called the cervix.

With the approach of adolescence, your ovaries begin to stir into action, prompted by hormones released in the brain. The first sign of the ovaries' activity is that every 28 days or so, one of your eggs starts to grow and mature and you begin to have periods. This is known as the menstrual cycle. This means that you have become sexually mature, and you are capable of having a baby.

Primary sexual organs
The reproductive organs are situated within the encircling pelvic bones. The uterus is a large pear-shaped, muscular organ that can expand to grow a baby and shrink back afterwards. The ovaries are glands that produce eggs and female hormones.

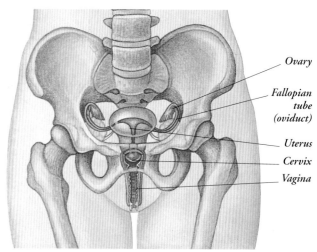

Ovary

Fallopian tube (oviduct)

Uterus

Cervix

Vagina

SECONDARY SEXUAL CHARACTERISTICS

Between the ages of about nine and 18, your body, under the influence of the female hormone oestrogen, changes from that of a child to that of a woman. A year or two before puberty at around nine or ten, the pelvic bones begin to grow and fat is deposited on the breasts, hips and thighs. In the adolescent phase, which starts from 11 to 16 years, your nipples start to bud, and pubic and underarm hair appears. At this stage, the genital organs develop and your periods will start. More fat is deposited on your hips, breasts and thighs. By the time you are 17 or 18 years old, bone growth will be complete.

The speed at which your body changes depends on many factors and it varies enormously from individual to individual, so don't worry if your friends are developing more quickly or more slowly than you.

Armpit hair At about 14 years, hair starts to grow in the armpits and the sweat glands become active.

Breasts The breasts begin to develop at about age 10 or 11. The area around the nipple (areola) becomes swollen and the nipple projects from its centre. Fat and glandular tissue within the breasts increase.

Skin Oestrogen affects the skin, causing more oil to be secreted. Some spots may appear.

Waist In contrast to broadening hips and breasts, the waist begins to look much more slender and defined.

Pubic hair Hair first appears on the labia at about 12 years and then gradually becomes thicker and curlier, spreading up to form a triangle shape. It may not match the colour of the hair on the head to begin with.

Thighs The inner and outer thighs develop pads of fat from about the age of 14, giving the body a more curvaceous, womanly outline.

Hips As the pelvic bones grow, the hips begin to broaden. Fat is laid down on the hips, helping to give the characteristic female shape.

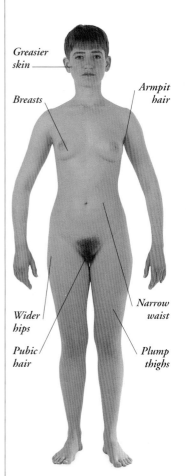

Greasier skin

Breasts

Armpit hair

Narrow waist

Wider hips

Pubic hair

Plump thighs

Physical development
Puberty begins about the age of 10 and lasts until 17 or 18. During this time, the female hormones produced by the ovaries change the shape of the girl from child to woman.

STARTING TO MENSTRUATE

No-one knows exactly why menstruation starts. What we do know is that it results from a coming together of many hormonal and chemical influences inside the body – from the brain, the adrenal glands, the ovaries and possibly from the thyroid gland. The age at which menstruation begins (the menarche) cannot be exactly anticipated, but it often follows a family pattern. If your mother started her periods early, then you are likely to, as well. For most of this century, girls have been starting to menstruate earlier and earlier, probably because of better nutrition, and today the average age of starting is around 11 years old. However, there is one general rule that has always applied – the younger you start your periods, the older you will be when you end them.

THE MENSTRUAL CYCLE

The menstrual cycle lasts on average about 28 days. Many girls experience a cycle that is exactly 28 days – a lunar cycle – but anything from 26 to 33 days is considered quite normal. The ovaries take turns to ovulate (produce an egg) each month. In the first half of your cycle, the maturing egg in the ovary produces mainly oestrogen. The primary effect of oestrogen at this time is on the uterus, where it causes the lining to thicken. Around the 14th day of your cycle (the first day of any cycle is counted as the day when you start to menstruate), the sac or follicle in the ovary containing the egg ruptures and the egg is released. It is immediately sucked up into the funnel-shaped end of one of the Fallopian tubes. Tiny microscopic hairs lining the tube move the egg into the uterus. This journey takes about three days. Unless the egg is fertilized by sperm on its way along the Fallopian tube, it dies.

Once the egg follicle has ruptured, the ovary begins to manufacture progesterone as well as oestrogen. Progesterone causes the lining of the uterus to become much thicker in preparation to receive a fertilized egg. It makes the breasts swell and the milk ducts and glands inside the breasts prepare for milk production in case fertilization takes place. That is why before your period your breasts may feel heavy and sore and your nipples may tingle. Progesterone also affects the skin, producing pimples, and many girls and women have a pimple or two on the face in the week before menstruation. At the same time, progesterone has an effect on vaginal discharge. In the first half of the month it is clear, thin and elastic, but under the action of progesterone it becomes thick, opaque, sticky and inelastic, with a different odour. All these changes in vaginal discharge are perfectly normal. It's abnormal to have no vaginal discharge at all. If it develops a strong odour, however, you may have an infection; you should consult a doctor.

WHY WE HAVE PERIODS

If fertilization and conception have not taken place by about the 25th day of your cycle, the egg dies and your ovaries stop producing both female hormones. This hormonal withdrawal causes the lining of the uterus, which has been thickening to receive the fertilized egg, to break down a few days later. Both the lining and the egg are expelled from the body, which you experience as bleeding. This usually lasts from three to seven days. The cycle then begins again with an ovary preparing to produce a new egg in readiness for conception.

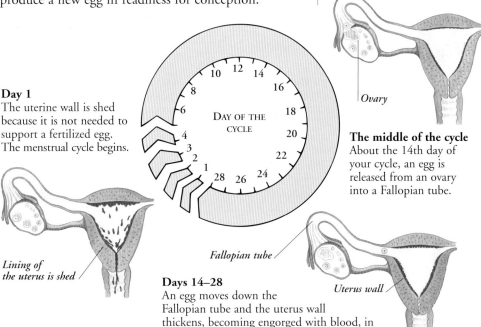

Day 1
The uterine wall is shed because it is not needed to support a fertilized egg. The menstrual cycle begins.

DAY OF THE CYCLE

Ovary

The middle of the cycle
About the 14th day of your cycle, an egg is released from an ovary into a Fallopian tube.

Lining of the uterus is shed

Fallopian tube

Days 14–28
An egg moves down the Fallopian tube and the uterus wall thickens, becoming engorged with blood, in anticipation of receiving a fertilized egg.

Uterus wall

TAMPON WITH APPLICATOR

REGULAR TAMPON

DAYTIME TOWEL WITH WINGS

NIGHT-TIME TOWEL

There is a rare infection called toxic shock syndrome (TSS), which is thought to be linked with wearing tampons. To avoid this, always use the least absorbent type of tampon to meet your needs, and never leave a tampon in for longer than eight hours. Always insert a clean one before going to bed.

Don't forget to remove the old tampon before putting in another, and if you ever "lose" a tampon, go straight to your doctor to have it removed.

YOUR FIRST PERIODS

When the periods begin, they are not usually bright red as you might expect; they tend to be rather brown and scant and they are hardly ever regular. At this stage, it's quite uncommon for a girl to have her period regularly every 30 days or so. Quite often in the beginning there are gaps of two, three or even six months between periods. It takes most girls a year or even 18 months to achieve regular monthly bleeding, so don't worry about initial irregularity, or a varying degree of blood loss, unless you might be pregnant. A few women never have regular periods. They go through life bleeding every three, five or even six weeks.

Reactions to periods The arrival of periods is a kind of coming of age – physically you're a woman, fertile and able to bear children, and so it should be a time of rejoicing. Each period should reaffirm your femininity, your individuality and your wholeness. Think of it as a confidence booster, not a cause of depression and feelings of inadequacy. Periods are, after all, an integral and regular part of life; you should value them because they're a symptom of how well your body is functioning. Try not to think of them as a big drag, even if you have symptoms such as discomfort, pain, bloatedness and lethargy. All of these symptoms can be treated quite easily.

The fact that many girls have mixed feelings about their periods is largely a legacy of Victorian attitudes. Synonyms for menstruation, such as "the curse", are remnants from Victorian times when all women's complaints were thought to be psychological, and women used to isolate themselves for about a week whenever they had a period. This is still so today in some cultures. Such attitudes are obviously unfair, especially since girls cannot control their hormonal cycles or their reactions to them. If your periods embarrass you, and you don't like to talk to your mother about them, the best thing to do is to talk with your sister or closest friend. Ask if she has started to menstruate and find out if she shares your feelings. Friends can sometimes help you over your embarrassment by their approach to things and it may help you put periods into perspective as a normal and acceptable part of life.

PROBLEM PERIODS

Girls often experience actual physical distress during their periods, the causes of which have been investigated and treatment is available. The two major conditions are painful periods (dysmenorrhoea) and PMS (pre-menstrual syndrome). Another problem some girls have is the complete lack of periods, known as amenorrhoea.

Dysmenorrhoea (painful periods) This means menstrual cramps, which can range from very mild to completely disabling. Once thought to be a neurotic condition, it is now known that it's all in our hormones – not in our heads. A girl who has very painful periods either secretes too much of the hormone prostaglandin, or her uterus is more sensitive than usual to normal amounts of it.

Prostaglandin is the hormone that triggers labour by causing the uterus to contract rhythmically and strongly enough to eject a baby. Girls (and women) who suffer from extremely painful periods must be taken seriously because they're going through a "mini-labour". You can help relieve the pain by taking ibuprofen, which can be bought over the counter at your pharmacy, or ask your doctor to prescribe mefenamic acid, which can relieve period pain and reduce blood loss.

Drugs containing anti-prostaglandins, which get to the root of the problem and bring relief in more than 80 percent of cases, are on the market in Great Britain, most European countries and the United States. The use of anti-prostaglandin has proved to be enormously helpful to many girls. It can shorten the time during which you feel pain and this reduces how long you have to stay in bed so that you can continue working at your studies or doing your job instead.

If you do have very painful periods and have not had an anti-prostaglandin prescribed, go to your doctor and ask whether you can be given one of these drugs. If your doctor refuses, go to a family planning clinic. If the doctor there is hesitant, ask for a referral to a gynaecologist.

PMS (Pre-menstrual Syndrome) Period pain and PMS are not related. PMS amounts, in many girls, to a great deal more than simply irritability, depression and a tendency to become tearful. It is a collection of

INSERTING A TAMPON

Trying out tampons for the first time can be tricky. Read the instructions in the packet first and relax.

1 Remove the wrapper by stripping the thread down one side. The outer tube holds the tampon, and the removal cord emerges from the open end of the plunger.

2 Relax the vagina by putting your foot on a raised surface. Hold the bottom of the outer tube and put your index finger on the end of the plunger.

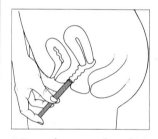

3 Insert the outer tube as high as you can into the vagina by pushing it upwards and backwards. When the tampon is inserted, the plunger is pushed up into the outer tube, expelling the tampon.

4 Pull in your vagina as tightly as possible and pull both tubes out together. Make sure that the string stays outside the vaginal opening.

HELP WITH MENSTRUAL PROBLEMS

One thing is certain, you should not have to suffer with your periods. If you do have problems, always seek medical advice from your doctor or from a family planning clinic doctor.

Research has shown that there are very clear physical causes for these complaints that should be tackled, rather than just suppressing the symptoms with tranquillizers, sedatives, hypnotics or antidepressants.

If you're not happy about some aspect of menstruation, don't keep problems and mixed-up feelings to yourself. First talk to your mother or guardian. If you find it difficult to communicate with your parents or you've never discussed sensitive subjects with them before, then you must look for help outside your family. You may have a sympathetic teacher, older female relative or neighbour to whom you feel close. Spill the beans to her; you must get your worries off your chest and get reassurance and advice. If you don't have anyone within the circle of your family or friends in whom you can confide, go to your doctor and try to be as frank as you can about your problems, or ask to see the nurse, who could also be a good source of informal help.

symptoms that varies from girl to girl, but for many, a number of the following symptoms occur regularly in the week before their periods:

- Headaches
- Arthritic pains
- Allergic symptoms
- Inability to concentrate
- Impatience and a quick temper
- A sense that the world is against you
- Physical clumsiness
- Inability to string words together or find a word
- Depression
- Sudden weight gain and bloating
- Insomnia

The cause of PMS is extremely complex; several organs and hormones are involved. Almost certainly, the hormone that causes water retention is produced in a higher quantity at this time and that is why diuretics (drugs that cause the body to eliminate water) sometimes help if bloating is the main symptom. In about half the girls who get depressed, there is a relative, and only relative, shortage of vitamin B6. This is why supplements of this vitamin can help depression. You should never take B6 supplements, however, without first seeing your doctor, because unsupervised medication can lead to very serious side-effects.

It is thought that PMS is probably caused by an imbalance of oestrogen- or progesterone-stimulating hormones from the brain, and some girls have this problem because they are short of progesterone. If this happens to you, replacement progesterone therapy with pessaries, injections or implants can help to relieve your symptoms.

Amenorrhoea This means absence of menstruation and apart from being a result of pregnancy, it is usually caused by metabolic diseases, chromosomal abnormalities or anorexia nervosa (see p. 24). It's normal for a girl still not to be menstruating by the age of 14, and many specialists would not dream of investigating this matter until a girl was 17, and only then after a thorough check-up. Tests can check that you have the right balance of hormones and the problem can be corrected with hormone replacement therapy.

2

GOOD HEALTH

Glowing skin, limitless energy and a positive outlook
are just a few of the benefits of being really healthy.
When you are eating well, exercising regularly
and getting plenty of rest, your weight will stabilize,
the condition of your skin, hair and nails will
improve and you'll feel on top of the world. Like
most of us, you've probably heard all sorts of
strange myths about exercise or about "good" or
"bad" foods, so in this chapter I set the record straight:
I explain how to make your diet healthier and
how to exercise sensibly. I also give you the facts
about drugs, alcohol and smoking, which can all
harm your health.

TAKING
RESPONSIBILITY
FOR YOUR DIET

If you are going to eat well, you must be prepared to take some of the initiative and responsibility for what you eat. You'll be doing your parents a big favour, as well as learning how to look after yourself if you:

• Make it your business to find out as much as you can about family meal planning and cooking.

• Help with or even do the family shop yourself. A by-product of this exercise would be that you learn all about budgeting and handling money, too.

Skin problems
If you have acne, a healthy diet is the best way to make sure that your skin, as well as your hair, nails and teeth are in good condition.

EATING WELL

Our diet has a lifelong effect on our health and general well-being. To look and feel good, we have to eat adequate amounts of the proper foods. Many teenagers, however, don't always choose the food that is best for their health. They may not want to eat what the rest of their family is having, and they may also eat poorly at school. By law, school meals must contain the correct nutrients to meet your needs, but if your school runs a cafeteria service where you can decide what you eat, the food you choose may not be nutritious enough. In fact, many teenagers prefer to eat fast food because it's easy.

CHOOSING GOOD FOOD

When given the freedom to choose their own meals, many teenagers opt for the quick take-out style of food, such as fish and chips, hamburgers, fried chicken or snacks such as chocolate bars, popcorn, biscuits or crisps. These are often referred to as "junk" foods, so named because they tend to be low in fibre, minerals and vitamins, and because they are often heavily processed and high in fats, sugar and calories. While it's definitely a bad idea to eat this type of food to the exclusion of all else, in the context of a varied, balanced diet, these foods often contain valuable nutrients (for example, a hamburger contains protein, iron, vitamins and minerals, although it is also high in fat). So it's perfectly all right to allow yourself the occasional treat of a take-out or some other snack food, but it's very important to build up good eating habits early on in life and to learn which foods are beneficial and which can have damaging effects. Choosing good foods will keep you in the best possible shape and as healthy as possible.

THE FOOD GROUPS

Proteins, carbohydrates, fats, minerals and vitamins are essential nutrients. As well as plenty of fibre, a balanced diet should contain at least the recommended quantities of all these essential foods. Doing without any one of them for a long time will lead to harmful effects and a disordered metabolism, and possibly to serious vitamin and mineral deficiencies, which may eventually lead to disease.

Proteins These are needed by the body to manufacture and repair tissues. They are the essential building materials of the body, used for muscle, skin, blood and nerves, so they're in constant demand. This means that you should eat 53–70 grams (2–2¾ ounces) of protein each day. Good sources include meat, fish, poultry, eggs, nuts, beans and dairy products.

Carbohydrates Carbohydrates in the form of unrefined rice and cereals, wholemeal bread, pasta, pulses, fresh fruit and vegetables (including potatoes and bananas) and wholegrains should make up about half our intake.

You should only eat processed carbohydrates, which include cakes, jams, chocolates, sweets and biscuits, in moderation, as part of a balanced diet. Our bodies use sugars from all sources (whether from cakes and biscuits or from fruit and milk) and each person's blood sugar level may vary from day to day and from hour to hour. If you consume too much sugar for your body's needs, you will store the excess as fat. So you should aim to include sugar from a whole range of sources and try to avoid adding extra sugar to your food.

Fats There are two types of fat, saturated fats, which are usually solid, such as butter, and unsaturated fats, which are usually liquid, such as oil. Saturated fats come from animal and dairy products and some vegetable oils including palm, coconut and palm kernel. Unsaturated fats are found in vegetable oils. High intakes of saturated fats in the diet are known to raise our cholesterol levels, which increases the risk of developing heart disease, and of suffering from stroke or circulation problems, so it is best to limit your consumption of saturated fats and include unsaturated fats in your diet.

A small amount of fat is necessary in our diet for the body to function normally. This means, for example, you need about 2 tablespoons (30ml) of salad oil per day – this could be olive, hazelnut, sesame seed or sunflower oil. Or you could reach this level of fat intake by adding nuts, avocados or mayonnaise to your diet. We should all eat lots of oily fish for their polyunsaturated fatty acids because they are linked to a lower risk of heart disease. Monounsaturated oils, such as olive and sesame, are preferable to saturated fats, such as lard, for cooking.

YOUR DAILY DIET

Your diet should provide plenty of nutrients to keep you healthy and full of energy, so you need to eat a combination of different foods every day.

Eat freely from the following:
- *Lean meat*
- *Poultry*
- *Fish*
- *Eggs*
- *Pulses (beans, peas or lentils)*
- *Bread, cereals, pasta, rice*
- *Fruit (apples, oranges, bananas, melon, peaches etc.)*
- *Vegetables (carrots, peas, broad beans, tomatoes, salad vegetables, green leafy vegetables etc.)*
- *Potatoes (not fried)*

Eat in moderation:
- *Dairy products (milk, cheese and yogurt)*
- *Nuts (including peanuts)*
- *Butter, margarine, jams and preserves*

Eat occasionally:
- *Cakes, biscuits, sweets, fizzy drinks, crisps, chips, popcorn*

A HEALTHIER DIET

Here are a few basic tips for eating a healthier diet. They are not difficult to follow, and should form the basis of your adult eating habits.

Try to cut down on:

• *Sugary food such as cakes, biscuits, sweets, chocolates and soft drinks. If you are used to eating snacks between meals, go for fruit, nuts, raisins or cheese.*

• *Fried and fatty foods if you eat them a lot. Have a poached or boiled egg instead of a fried one, and grill your meat whenever you can. Baked potatoes are better than chips as they contain a lot less fat.*

• *Refined foods. Replace them with fresh foods instead. Reduce the amount of white bread products you eat and have more wholewheat products, which not only contain more protein and vitamins but more fibre.*

Fibre Fibre in the diet has been discussed a great deal over the last few years. We now know that fibre absorbs water, helping both to stave off hunger pangs and to keep the colon healthy by making bowel motions regular and soft. Fibre has an important role in protecting us from certain diseases, such as heart disease, and some cancers and bowel conditions. It can be found in all foods of plant origin, the most important sources being unrefined breads, rice and pasta, cereals, vegetables and starchy roots such as potatoes, pulses, such as peas and beans, and nuts and fruit. Cellulose and pectin, found in all stringy vegetables and fruit cannot be digested, but they are vital as roughage.

Minerals Two of the most important minerals are calcium and iron. Calcium is essential for the proper growth of bones and teeth, while iron is required for healthy blood, particularly for women who menstruate. Also, because you are growing fast during your teenage years and your blood volume increases, you may need extra iron. You can get iron from meat, shellfish, offal, eggs and watercress. Other essential minerals including sodium, potassium, zinc, iodine and fluoride, which you need in tiny amounts, will be provided by a balanced healthy diet, as long as it includes meat or fish, vegetables, grains and fruits.

Calcium is found in milk and dairy products such as yogurt and cheese. It's especially important for young women in their teens and early twenties, when peak bone mass is reached, to combine a calcium-rich diet with vitamins A and D, and to exercise to build strong bones. The risk of developing osteoporosis (brittle

Fresh vegetables
Eating more fresh vegetables, which are packed with vitamins, minerals and fibre, is one of the best ways of improving your daily diet.

bones) in later life depends on your bone mass. Around half of all teenage girls don't take enough calcium – and many don't exercise at all (see p. 22).

Vitamins   These are essential to regulate your body processes. Vitamin A is needed for healthy vision and maintaining body tissues. The best sources of vitamin A are yellow and orange vegetables, dark-green vegetables and some fats. Vitamin C is used in many body processes, including healing, and is needed for the absorption of iron. Unlike some of the other vitamins, vitamin C cannot be stored in the body, so you need a regular daily intake. Good sources are citrus fruits and dark green vegetables. Vitamin B^{12} is found mainly in meat and offal, eggs, dairy products and some cereals. The best sources of vitamin D are oily fish, eggs and some cereals.

MAINTAINING A HEALTHY WEIGHT

Many teenage girls go through phases of being very worried about their weight. They may feel that they're too fat all over, or they may just feel that they're too fat in some places. A girl who is ten percent or more over her ideal weight is overweight, but if she is 20 percent or more above the ideal, it indicates that she is obese. So according to these criteria, around half of adults over 20 may be overweight, and it is a serious problem for many.

It used to be assumed that if a child was overweight, the fat would vanish at maturity. But today surplus fat is thought to be a problem at whatever age it occurs. However, weighing yourself daily and taking measurements will not always tell you whether you are overweight. You must look at your frame and decide whether you are small-, medium- or large-framed. If you have a large frame, you will need more flesh to cover you than if you are small-framed, and you will consequently weigh more.

Also, at your stage of life, your weight may fluctuate – you may well be still growing, for one thing – and you may also weigh more when you are premenstrual. So it's not a good idea just to focus on your weight, but to look at your overall shape. If you are still serious about losing weight, write this energy equation on your mirror:

Accumulation of body fat = food taken in
minus the energy used by the body

HEALTHY EATING

As part of your new eating plan, make your diet healthier by adding these:

● *Try to eat five servings of fresh fruit or vegetables each day. The best way to cook vegetables is to steam them – they lose less of their goodness that way. Whenever you can, eat raw vegetables.*

● *Drink skimmed or semi-skimmed milk rather than full fat milk – all the essential ingredients of milk are still present after most of the fat has been removed.*

● *Add peas, beans, lentils and pulses to your diet whenever you can. They provide good protein very cheaply and contain a lot of fibre.*

● *Eat more wholegrain products. There are now many wholemeal breads and kinds of wholemeal pasta available; brown rice is better than white rice and has a much nicer flavour and texture. Make your own sandwiches with wholemeal bread instead of buying those made from white bread.*

● *Anorexia and even dieting can make a girl vulnerable to brittle bones in later life – and much earlier than a girl who eats normally.*

DIETING RULES

Remember, any successful diet involves consuming fewer calories and eating less food. You're fooling yourself if you think a diet that permits you to eat anything you want will help you to lose weight. To lose weight follow these simple rules:

- *Don't eat a large meal in the evening when you'll have little opportunity for exercise afterwards. It's best to eat more at the times when you are going to be most active.*

- *Eat a hearty breakfast, a substantial lunch and then a light supper.*

- *Eat slowly and chew the food thoroughly.*

- *Don't eat while you're doing anything else, such as reading or watching television. Give eating your full attention.*

- *Put your food on to smaller plates – less will seem more.*

- *Stop frying altogether – grilling is healthier and can be just as tasty.*

- *Drink skimmed or semi-skimmed milk. The cream in regular milk contains too many calories anyway. All the nutrients are in what's left.*

- *If you must snack, stock up the fridge with low-calorie nibbles and snacks like low-fat yogurt and raw vegetables.*

- *Throw away left-over fattening food, or put it in the freezer – don't leave it in the fridge where you can nibble at it between meals.*

When, for whatever reason, your food intake is higher than your energy output, you have an excess that is stored as fat. The reverse happens when output outstrips intake; fat becomes a source of energy, it is burnt up, and weight is lost. If you really want to get slim and stay trim, you should pay close attention to the equation. There are no shortcuts and there is no easy way out. You can only reduce your body fat if you eat less or exercise more, or preferably, a combination of both.

When you are on a diet you naturally pay a lot of attention to your food intake, but your energy expenditure is also crucial, and you should aim to raise it and keep it up. There are certain influences that can affect the balance of the energy equation. One of these is your basal metabolic rate (BMR), the measurement of the amount of food energy that your body uses to fuel all the functions essential for life and health, such as breathing and digestion. It accounts for about two-thirds of the body's energy needs and is linked to how much muscle we have.

When planning to lose weight, most girls opt for cutting down what they eat because they can lose weight quickly this way; but it's more beneficial to increase your amount of exercise, because this can affect the energy equation just as quickly and, importantly, more effectively, in the long term.

Exercising to lose weight Recently we've discovered that exercise not only affects the energy equation in a more subtle way than through direct expenditure of energy, but that regular exercise is, in fact, the only way we know of altering our BMR. If you exercise enough to become fit – that is, four times a week for 30 minutes or longer, over a period of months – muscles become stronger and body fat is burnt off. Exercising muscle has about twice the BMR of fat and resting muscle, so the body adapts and prepares for the increased work done by the heart, lungs and muscles by "ticking over" or metabolizing at a slightly higher rate, thereby using more energy even on those days when you do not exercise.

This makes exercise one of the most valuable slimming aids we have. In fact, it is the only dieting aid that has come to light in recent years that gets to the root of weight control. Despite this, few dieters understand the importance of exercise or put it to full use.

If you are too thin Being underweight is a difficult problem to deal with because most girls who are thin have a high metabolic rate for many reasons, and it's very hard to slow the rate down. If you are persistent, you can actually put on weight but you will have to eat several large meals a day containing fattening foods and you must never miss a meal. It's now fashionable to be thin, but being too slender can be unhealthy and lead to serious eating disorders (see p. 24). Height/weight tables used for life insurance purposes have recently been revised upwards because it's now known that people who are up to 4kg (8lb) above their recommended weight are likely to live longer than those who are this much underweight.

If you are overweight Many girls embarking on a slimming campaign have quite unrealistic expectations of how much weight they are likely to lose and how quickly. They get depressed about dieting and soon give up. It's essential, therefore, that you understand what losing weight is all about before you start on a diet. Naturally, your weight loss depends on how many calories you go without. If your average calorie needs are 2,000 per day, even a fairly generous diet of 1,500 calories creates an energy deficit of 500 calories per day or 3,500 per week, which is the equivalent in energy terms of 0.5kg (1lb) of body fat.

Crash dieting Crash dieting is a very bad way of losing weight in the long run because although the amount of weight you lose straight away is likely to be impressive, and may be as much as 5kg (10lb) in the first week, less than half of this will be fat, which is what you're aiming to lose. If you reduce your food intake to, say, 400 calories a day, roughly half the initial weight reduction will be because of water loss. Cutting down your food like this is really low-grade starvation; all you'll do is gradually put your body into a state of hibernation – it will turn down the fuel burners to conserve energy and to stay alive. Once in this state, it's impossible to lose weight because your needs may be as little as 500 calories a day, and you'll find that you don't have enough energy to keep going normally. If you want to lose weight permanently, you must revamp your whole style of eating and activity levels.

CHOOSING A DIET

If you decide that you want to go on a diet, do a bit of personal research. No-one but you can tell which diet is best suited to you. When choosing a diet you should bear in mind that you're accepting a new pattern of eating for the rest of your life, so here are a few questions to ask yourself:

- *Is my diet flexible? Any good diet must be so, because few girls lead lives so well organized that they can stick rigidly to a specific menu for any length of time.*

- *Is my diet too strict? You can't expect to exist on much less than 1,000 calories a day.*

- *Are the diet's permitted foods acceptable to me? It's fatal to choose a diet that suggests eating a lot of something you don't like or rarely eat.*

- *Does my diet allow a few small indulgences? Most people can stick to a diet more easily if it allows them to have a treat now and then.*

- *If I am living at home, will my diet fit in with what the family eats? Can I enlist my Mum's help?*

- *Is the diet nutritionally well balanced? You should not try fad diets. Any diet which involves eating only one or two foods is unhealthy.*

- *Is the diet expensive? High-protein diets may fall into this category – fillet steak is rarely within a teenager's or her family's budget.*

EATING DISORDERS

Most children develop certain likes and dislikes from quite an early age and, depending on how their parents react, these fads either linger into adulthood or disappear. If you get to your teens and you have strong food dislikes, it's quite likely that your parents have, in a sense, encouraged you by focusing too much attention on your eating habits. This is OK as long as you do not become obsessive about what you eat – a "faddy" eater. When young adults are like this it is annoying, insensitive to others, and even dangerous if you start a faddy diet, go too far and begin to cut out essential nutrients. Taken to extremes, there are "slimmers' diseases" where food fads have far more deep-seated causes.

Anorexia nervosa This sometimes fatal disease is believed to result from psychological causes, and recent research has shown that anorexia can run in families. However, it's not known whether it's genetic or whether sufferers merely copy their mothers' eating habits. Anorexia is much commoner than we think: about ten percent of all teenage girls have it in one form or another, although some of them only have it in a very mild form.

The disease nearly always starts in the early teenage years, although a significant and worrying number of younger children are affected too. It usually begins with a girl trying to lose weight and get "slim". But often the girl is subconsciously trying to show that she is in control of her life and that her parents or guardians are not. Some girls may also be subconsciously wanting to remain a child and be fighting against their developing bodies by trying to slim down and keep themselves "childlike". Managing their eating is an easy way for girls to take control of themselves. Those in authority around her or those looking after her may be fooled into thinking that they control her eating habits as well, but

Confused self-image
Many girls who are thin but anorexic see a distortion of their actual body shape when they look in the mirror (right).

they don't realize that a girl will use all sorts of ploys to make sure that very little food actually gets into her body, including forcing herself to vomit.

It's amazing the lengths that some girls will go to to achieve their desired shape. Whatever the initial cause, anorexic girls develop an unrealistic idea of what their body is like. When asked to draw their shape, they nearly always represent it as a kind of Michelin man – they think they're far too fat and even though they may be 170cm (5ft 7in) tall and weigh only 41.3kg (6½ stones), they would still like to be thinner. They are absolutely terrified of regaining the weight they have lost and getting "fat". They will go for days existing on no more than cups of tea, using saccharin sweeteners.

Many anorexics suffer serious side-effects as well as getting very thin. Their hair starts to fall out, their periods dwindle and even stop, and they may also start growing unsightly body hair. They may also go on to develop osteoporosis (brittle bones) in later life. In some extreme cases, the girl dies.

For a girl to overcome anorexia, she has to undergo a profound change inside herself. She has to put aside any desire to remain childlike, with non-existent breasts and no periods, and come to terms with approaching adult-hood and all its responsibilities. Far and away the best help is to meet other anorexics through self-help groups which will offer advice, support and information.

BULIMIA

This is thought to be a variation of anorexia nervosa (see left).

Those who suffer from this condition usually go for several days with very little food and then become crazed with an uncontrollable desire for food so that they eat almost anything in sight which is edible. This may mean eating extraordinary mixtures of raw and cooked food, sweet and savoury mixed in huge quantities. Some women have died after such a "binge" because their stomachs have ruptured under the strain. Some women eat normally but then force themselves to vomit immediately afterwards. This pattern of starving, bingeing and vomiting is very hard to break. It's also much more common than people think, but drugs can help this condition.

A GIRL'S IDEAL WEIGHT

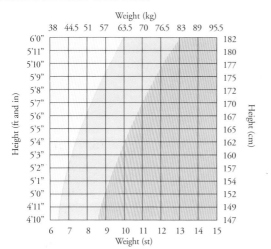

Weight (kg)

Underweight

Acceptable weight

Overweight

Your weight
Check what your ideal weight should be from the chart (left). It shows an "acceptable" weight range for each height that covers the normal variation in body shape. However, if you are small-framed, your ideal weight should be nearer the lower range.

REST AND SLEEP

Every living organism, whether plant or animal, takes a period of rest after a growth or activity cycle. We probably need more rest than any other animal because our level of activity is so varied. We have more complicated bodies and more complex brains, which undertake the kind of thinking and sifting of information that is unique to humankind. All human beings need a period of rest within each 24 hours.

THE NEED TO SLEEP

Such is the activity of our brains that very often by the end of 16 hours of activity the brain cells are completely depleted of energy necessary for brain activity. After eight or so hours of rest, however, one finds that the same brain cells are completely recharged with large, plump energy granules, ready for the day ahead. Only sleep will refurbish brain cells. It's logical to assume that all the cells in our body and our metabolic processes need this kind of daily replenishing process for growth and repair.

Sleep is a very complicated process and the brain has at least two centres that are involved in our ability to sleep; one makes us go to sleep and the other keeps us asleep. The first centre is triggered by a variety of factors, for example, habit, what is going on around us, and physical and mental tiredness. It's thought that the second centre is triggered by chemical reactions occurring in the body and brain cells once we are asleep.

Directed by the brain, every organ in the body goes into neutral when we're asleep. The heartrate slows down, the body's temperature drops and breathing becomes very slow, which means that the body is relatively short of oxygen. So you can think of the body as being in a state of partial hibernation when you're asleep.

DREAMING

The body can only recover from a day's activity through rest and sleep, but most sleep scientists believe that it is through dreaming that the brain restores and prepares itself for the next day. We all dream even though we may not remember our dreams. Think of your brain as a computer which has to absorb, channel, sift, analyse and synthesize information constantly. It's pretty obvious

Your sleep routine
Set your alarm clock for the same time every day; sleeping in can upset your body's natural rhythm, making it much harder to get up the next morning.

that if the brain cells have become clogged with too much information, a fuse will blow or everything will slow down unless you can clear it by having a good night's sleep during which you dream.

TIPS FOR SLEEPING WELL

So important is it that you get sufficient sleep that I think that you could try a few of the following things to encourage sleep each night, even if normally you don't have much trouble getting to sleep:

• You'll sleep more easily and more deeply if you are physically tired; so make sure that you get enough exercise each day.

• Make sure that your bedroom is well ventilated and at a comfortable temperature. The best combination is a coolish room with a warm bed.

• Wear comfortable pyjamas or a nightdress; avoid constricting clothing.

• Make sure that your feet aren't cold.

• Just before going to bed, try to do something that you find relaxing. It may be taking a warm bath, or reading a few chapters of a good book.

• Have a warm drink at bedtime, but not one that contains stimulants such as tea or coffee.

• Eat something. A little food in the stomach diverts blood away from the brain and makes you feel drowsy, but avoid eating a heavy meal last thing at night.

• Try not to sleep in for too long at the weekend because this will disturb your normal sleep routine.

• Go to bed half an hour before you want to go to sleep, to allow yourself time to wind down.

• Try to follow a personal relaxation routine just before you go to sleep, for example:

1 Think about each part of your body in turn and tense it, then relax it.

2 Slow down your breathing by taking one long breath in and out in the time you would normally take two shallow breaths.

3 Try relaxing your mind to stop it racing. Empty it completely of thoughts; think about black velvet or simply concentrate on your breathing. Every time a negative thought creeps in, say "no", and concentrate on your breathing. There's a lot of good sense in "counting sheep".

Get involved in sports
Playing a sport, such as basketball, outside in the fresh air is one of the best ways of guaranteeing a good night's sleep.

EXERCISE FOR HEALTH

Exercise will benefit almost every aspect of your life. If you keep your figure trim and toned, and your weight at the proper level, your looks will improve. Agility, suppleness and gracefulness look great, and these, along with energy and strength, are the result of exercise. On top of this, most forms of exercise give you a chance to make friends and to enjoy yourself, as well as making you feel positive about yourself, relaxed and refreshed.

To keep your body trim and in good shape, you should try to take some form of exercise every other day or at least four times a week. It can be any sort of exercise, but it's best if it's the type that you really enjoy rather than having to endure an activity that you don't. If you walk a mile at a brisk pace every day, or swim, cycle or play any sports several times a week, you will increase your body's efficiency and stamina. You will gradually become less breathless after exertion because the fitness of your heart will improve.

"I started off on an indoor bike but it was so boring. Now I go out in all weathers and cycle near my home."

The more vigorous forms of exercise not only keep you fit but use up quite a few calories, too. At each session you should warm up gently and then exercise for at least 20 minutes, but it's better if you can do 30 minutes or more. It has to be fairly active – enough to make you pant and sweat a little – to be of real use.

Regular exercise has several real benefits. First, your body is working the way it is meant to, and this means it will be able to perform for you if you need to draw on extra reserves in an emergency. It will also give you a wonderful sense of well-being, probably because of the release of hormones such as endorphins, that are the body's natural painkillers and anti-depressants. Regular exercise helps everything to become easier (mentally as well as physically) and it also helps prevent you from putting on weight because your body raises its BMR (basal metabolic rate) to cope with the increased exercise load and to keep all your exercised muscles fully energized even when at rest (see p. 22).

Stretching to warm up
To avoid injury, always stretch before you exercise. With your feet wide apart, bend each knee in turn, keeping the other leg straight; you'll feel a pull in your inner thighs.

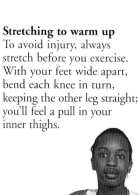

Types of exercise It's important to choose a form of exercise that you enjoy, that suits you and fits in with your lifestyle. It's pointless, say, to take up jogging in the early morning if you know you loathe getting up earlier than you have to. So you have to decide – do you like sport and playing games with other people? Or do you prefer to do something on your own, in your own time? It's up to you.

There are many sports and activities that provide all-round exercise. If you're keen on team sports such as netball, basketball, volleyball, tennis or badminton, join a club or sports centre where you can play for fun as well as competitively. Dancing is an excellent exercise – if you've been doing ballet classes, keep them going even if you don't want to take it up seriously; or join a jazz or contemporary dance group; even tap or line dancing can be energetic. Aerobics or "step" classes exercise the whole body and are fun to do with a group of friends. All these activities are not only good for your general fitness, but also help strengthen the long bones of your legs and help contribute to the development of peak bone mass, which is important if you want to avoid developing brittle bones later on.

If you don't want to take exercise in a formal setting, there are plenty of ways you can still get in shape. You could incorporate a walk into your daily routine; try walking to school instead of catching the bus. Walk fairly briskly but not jerkily, and keep up a continuous, easy pace. Your circulation will improve and your heart and lungs will be stimulated. Wear comfortable shoes, even if it means carrying a spare pair with you to change into. If it's too far to walk, use your bicycle if you've got one. Cycling is excellent for your legs and for toning up your whole body in general. Running is good for your heart and lungs, and it will also keep you toned up. You'll need to set aside a time each day to run, and wear the appropriate running shoes that provide support and are geared to the type of terrain you'll be running over. Swimming is also an ideal all-round exercise and you'll notice your standard improving very quickly if you swim regularly. Apart from gently toning up all your muscles without the risk of straining yourself, swimming also helps your breathing and circulation.

Yoga
Start yoga or a stretch routine to improve your strength and muscle tone as well as to relax you mentally and physically.

"Exercise makes me feel so good for the rest of the day; I'm addicted to it."

SMOKING AND ALCOHOL

Very often, young people start to smoke just because they are curious to find out for themselves what smoking feels like. They may carry on experimenting for several years before they get hooked on it, but usually smoking becomes addictive very quickly, and is one of the hardest habits to break. It is also one of the most damaging to your health. Smoking is an abnormal and unnatural habit and nearly all regular smokers become dependent on the nicotine in cigarettes. There is plenty of evidence to show that the habit often leads to serious illness and early death. The main risks of death are from lung cancer and heart disease. In addition, smoking causes a great deal of misery and days off sick due to peptic ulcers and emphysema and other breathing problems. No sensible person would ignore these terrible risks, but millions of heavy smokers do.

"It just struck me one day what a crazy thing to be doing, and it costs so much money anyway."

Most young people smoke to be like adults or because they're afraid of being different from their friends who are smoking for that reason. Many teenage girls also take up smoking because they think it will keep their weight down; you may have seen fashion models smoking and want to be like them. If your parents smoke, you're more likely to take up smoking than if they don't. You may also begin to smoke because people you admire such as actors or rock stars do. However, it's infinitely more mature to resist the pressure to smoke and decide to stay a non-smoker.

Why start to smoke?
It is a known fact that smoking will damage your health and shorten your life – it also costs a great deal of money over the years.

Stopping or never starting You will be more likely to resist smoking if adults who you respect, such as parents, teachers, sports coaches or youth counsellors, don't smoke. At one time smoking was considered normal behaviour in homes, offices, on public transport and even in cinemas and theatres. Now it's becoming a much more anti-social habit as rules and regulations about smoking in these places are becoming stricter.

Even if you feel that the health risks of smoking are too remote to affect you, bear in mind that smoking makes you less attractive. A lot of people now feel that smoking is quite repugnant and this will put them off you from the outset. Your hair and clothes will smell of stale cigarettes and your breath will, too.

"I started because everyone else in our family smokes and my brother who is only a year older smokes."

Remind yourself of the following facts whenever you feel like having a cigarette. Even a smoker who smokes no more than 15 cigarettes a day will probably forfeit five and a half years of her life. Every cigarette you smoke costs you four minutes of your life. In fact, the difference in lifespan between men and women is now shrinking because women are smoking a lot more than they used to; there's a rising toll of women succumbing to lung cancer, the most rapidly fatal cancer. One more thing to bear in mind is that should you ever plan to have children, one out of every ten babies of a smoking mother is lost through miscarriage, or dies soon after birth. Mothers who smoke usually have babies who are smaller and lighter than those of non-smokers, and they run greater risks of having a premature baby. Their children may also develop asthma.

"I really felt left out if I wasn't smoking – I wasn't one of the crowd. And anyway, they all said I was pathetic because I was the only one that wasn't smoking."

If you feel that you are becoming addicted to smoking, try to talk to your parents about it, especially if you're having trouble refusing offered cigarettes or have begun to buy them yourself. They are likely to have some useful advice about how to say "no".

ALCOHOL

Drinking alcohol is another of those activities that you may think of as being "mature" because you see adults doing it. While a small amount of alcohol may be pleasant and sociable, it's important to bear in mind that it can be both a drug and a poison. It's so readily available that it's all too easy to get into the habit of drinking regularly with your friends, and for alcohol to become first a small habit and, in time, a big one. In the long term, alcohol ravages the body, completely destroying the liver, so that alcoholics experience liver failure and die, and a most unpleasant death it is. What's more, in the later stages of alcoholism their brains become "pickled" so that intellectual ability plummets. Drinking is becoming more and more common among young people because it's easy to get hold of and is a fairly cheap way of making yourself feel good. However, many young people don't know when to stop drinking once they've started. You might feel you're just going to have a drink or two to be sociable, but then find that the drink has already affected you enough to make you unable to stop there. It's also extremely easy to be persuaded by friends to have "just one more". The reality is that any "high" you get from alcohol lasts a very short time and is often followed by a very unpleasant hangover. You may experience quite bad depression as well as a splitting headache.

"I'd do anything for a drink, I'd steal and cheat. I've even stolen money out of my Mum's bag."

Treating alcohol with respect No-one can stop you drinking if you really are determined to, but remember that you are taking a risk every time you take a drink. In any event, you are not allowed to drink alcohol in pubs or wine bars in this country until you are 18, though you may go into bars with someone who is over 18 and drink soft drinks while you are still under age. Whatever else you do, never drink and drive, and never let anyone who has been drinking drive you, no matter how capable they insist they are. Another point to consider is that alcohol affects your behaviour and impairs your judgement. You may find that "under the influence" you've allowed yourself to do things that you bitterly regret afterwards.

"Oh, everybody drinks, adults get plastered, so why shouldn't we?"

How your parents can help Since drinking is such a widespread social activity, and something about which you will have to make up your own mind, the best place to learn about it is at home.

Most parents should be willing to consider letting you have a taste of any alcohol served at home, though as the law stands, they should not really be letting you have alcohol before the age of 18. They should also be able to discuss any problems you encounter – such as what to do about getting home if you're with someone who's been drinking, or what to do if your friends go to pubs or wine bars regularly and you're finding it difficult to refuse a drink.

DRUG-TAKING

The drug-taking scene was changed dramatically by the dance culture of the early 1980s when ecstasy burst into the lives of young people, replacing alcohol as an accompaniment to raves and clubbing. The "dance" drugs like amphetamine, LSD and ecstasy gained ground and the dangerous practice of taking a cocktail of several different drugs became more and more prevalent. Several young people have now died after taking just one tablet of ecstasy.

CANNABIS

Cannabis has never been a dance drug. It's not really addictive, and on its own it does much less harm than cigarettes – the first death from cannabis has yet to be recorded, while thousands die every year from alcohol and cigarettes. However, many people smoke cannabis with tobacco, which may lead to nicotine addiction, and cannabis smoke contains more tar than tobacco. There is also evidence that heavy cannabis use can lead to short-term memory loss and no-one should drive while under its influence.

Contrary to what many people think, cannabis is not a "gateway drug" to harder drugs like heroin or cocaine. Alcohol and tobacco are the gateway drugs and those who escalate to hard drugs would probably have taken hard drugs whether they'd smoked cannabis or not. Cannabis is, however, illegal and stays in the body for some time. Repeated use is therefore cumulative.

THE DANGER OF TAKING DRUGS

All illegal drugs, except cannabis, can be very dangerous. No-one swallowing an ecstasy tablet can know exactly what is in it – often they're "spiked" with dangerous chemicals. The body's reaction to an illegal drug is therefore completely unpredictable. People who take more than one dose or tablet, and who combine drugs, are asking for trouble because they are dramatically multiplying the chances of having a bad reaction.

Few drug-takers have any idea of safety precautions or what basic first aid may be needed if something goes wrong (see column, right). Did you know, for instance, that if someone has taken ecstasy and is dancing, it's

FIRST AID FOR DRUGS

If someone you're with has problems when on drugs, stay with her (or him).

• *If she's panicking – take her to a quiet place and stay with her until she's calmed down. Try to get her to breathe deeply and slowly – get her to copy you.*

• *If she's being sick while lying down, make her sit or stand up with her head down.*

• *If she is unconscious, loosen her clothing and lay her in the recovery position. If you know how to do CPR (resuscitation) be prepared to do it.*

• *Get medical help as soon as possible by calling an ambulance or speaking to first aid or security staff. Tell the paramedics exactly what your friend has taken – you may save her life.*

SAYING NO TO DRUGS

If drug-taking friends try to make you feel like a freak because you won't join in, remember that there are plenty of other people who feel like you do. It's not cool to do drugs – it's dangerous and illegal.

- *Remember that you always have a choice – say no.*

- *Avoid places where drugs are available.*

- *Make some new friends who don't take drugs.*

- *Focus on something positive that makes you feel really good about yourself, such as your studies or a sport.*

- *Look after your body and take regular exercise – it boosts self-esteem and gives you a natural high.*

important that they sip about 250ml (½ pint) of water every half hour – not 2 litres (3½ pints) all in one go which could kill? They should also not wear a hat, and rest (chill out) regularly. Get informed to be able to help a friend.

DRUG FACTS

A detailed discussion on drugs is beyond the scope of this book, but there are useful books and contact numbers available (see p. 126). I've included here some points that might help you weigh things up carefully.

You may think that you know exactly how you feel about drugs. You may have seen friends getting high and decided that, next time you get the chance, you're going to try it too. You may be someone who hates the idea of losing control, so much so that you're determined never to act that way – even if it makes you feel like an outsider at times. Or you may be in two minds: sitting on the fence and weighing up the good and bad points, and wondering which way to jump. The best way to explore your feelings about drugs is to find out everything you can about them, and arm yourself with the facts.

Here are some important facts:
- Taking drugs and being in possession of drugs are illegal activities; you can go to prison if you're caught.
- Taking drugs can be extremely dangerous; drugs can kill you.
- You could become dependent on drugs.
- Taking drugs is a leap in the dark; you can never be sure what's in a dose.
- Drugs mess with your mind and body.
- One bad experience can leave permanent damage.
- You always have to come down. The higher you go, the harder you fall.
- If you're mentally unstable, drugs will make your condition worse.

Drugs and the law Almost all recreational drugs are illegal and carry heavy penalties. Even being found in possession of one ecstasy tablet or a tiny amount of cannabis could result in a prison sentence if you're prosecuted and found guilty by a law court. So remember: using drugs, having drugs in your possession, giving drugs away, buying drugs or selling drugs may mean going to jail and getting a prison record.

CHAPTER 3

LOOKING GOOD

When we are bombarded daily with images of stunning
supermodels, it's easy to feel inadequate about our looks.
I believe the key to looking good is to learn how to
enhance your best features; you may have gorgeous eyes, for
example, or pretty hair, long legs, an attractive smile or a
tiny waist. Your teens are a brilliant time to experiment
with make-up, hairstyles and clothes. Magazines can be
sources of inspiration and you'll probably enjoy swopping
clothes and make-up with friends to discover what's
right for you. I also believe that you are never too
young to start taking care of your complexion, teeth
and nails: it is one of the best investments you can
make for the future.

GOOD SKIN

No girl growing up these days should feel that she ought to conform to media models – it's worth remembering that one of the reasons models and stars look attractive in photographs or on screen is through technological trickery, clever lighting, and make-up, and that they may look much less attractive from another angle. Being yourself and believing in yourself are your most powerful sources of self-respect, and this applies to the way you look as well as the way you think.

You've got to accept that you're made the way you are, and that you must make the most of what you've got and try to turn your minuses into pluses. We're all different and it's those differences that make us unique, valuable individuals. Forget about what you think you ought to look like. Learn to live with yourself as you are.

LOOKING AFTER YOUR SKIN

A really great-looking skin is a big plus and one of your most important assets. So whether you were born with a perfect complexion, or one that is not so good, you should make an effort to take care of it properly. When you are going through adolescence, your body is trying to sort out its hormone balance, and this affects your skin.

Spots Never squeeze spots because this spreads the infection into the deeper layers of the skin. You can squeeze uninflamed blackheads after a hot bath or shower, when all the pores are open, but afterwards apply a small dab of antiseptic cream to keep the skin clear. Don't use over-the-counter spot cream, and if your skin is very oily, refrain from using an abrasive cleanser – this simply spreads the bacteria.

Acne Nearly every teenager has acne at some stage. During adolescence high levels of sex hormones are secreted, which lead to the production of large quantities of sebum in the skin. Sebum is an irritant that may block the pores causing a purplish lump, which may become infected and form a pustule. One or two pimples are only to be expected but severe acne tends to scar, so ask your doctor for an acne preparation to help clear it. There are many good ones, but you'll need a prescription.

DRY SKIN

Dry skin looks dry, sometimes flakes and often feels taut, particularly if you've washed it with soap and water.

It is sometimes short of protective sebum and reacts to very hot or very cold weather by tightening up. One benefit is that dry skin is less likely to develop pimples than oily skin. However, it easily becomes chapped or roughened in a dry atmosphere.

- *Always use mild, alcohol-free make-up and toner and a rich, creamy cleanser.*

- *Moisturize your face as often as you can, including the throat and the skin around your eyes. Be lavish with it.*

- *When you wear make-up, use a moisturized foundation.*

- *Use little or no powder.*

COMBINATION SKIN

Most of us have this kind of skin, with an oily centre panel or a T-zone across the forehead, nose and chin, and areas of dryness on the cheeks, and around the eyes and neck.

- *Ideally, you should have one product for the oily areas and one for the dry areas, but this is expensive and unnecessary unless the contrast is very marked. It's simpler to use a milky cleanser.*

- *Use a skin tonic for the central oily panel, diluted with water for the drier areas.*

- *The drier areas may need moisturizing quite frequently.*

Cleaning the skin Cleanse or wash most parts of your body once a day, and your genital area more often if you possibly can. Cleansing your face doesn't mean you have to wash with soap and water; there are many simple, inexpensive cleansing creams in the shops. Whichever method you use, cleanse your skin sufficiently for it to feel clean. Some girls say that their skin does not feel clean unless it's washed with soap and water, well that's fine too. Be sure to find out what suits you first and foremost.

Using a moisturizer Moisturizing your skin is the single most important thing that you can do for it, and the earlier you start, the better. Up to the age of 20, a light, fluffy moisturizing cream applied after you wash or cleanse your face, morning and evening, is fine. Soaking for a long time in a hot bath is a bad idea as it washes away oils in the skin, making it feel dry afterwards. Whenever possible, take a shower instead, but if you do take baths, only stay in for a short time.

Cleansing and moisturizing Remove eye make-up carefully with an eye make-up remover pad or cleansing lotion, drawing it gently outwards across the lids. Do not stretch the skin.

Work a generous amount of cleansing lotion into your face with your fingertips. Use cotton wool or facial tissues to remove it. If you prefer to cleanse with soap and water, use a detergent-free cleansing bar and work up a good lather. Rinse thoroughly to remove all traces.

To refresh your skin, smooth a little toner over your face. Leave out your lips and eyes as it could irritate them.

To finish, dot moisturizing lotion generously over your whole face using the fingertips. Slowly smooth the moisturizer all over your complexion. Work from the centre outwards. Work into the crevices around the eyes, but be careful not to stretch the skin.

Skin types There are three basic skin types, but you may find that yours isn't exactly like any of those described in this book, or in any other. Most skins are a mixture of types and yours will be no exception. The three basic skin types are dry, oily and combination (see columns). Dark skins have a tendency towards greater extremes of dryness and oiliness than paler skins.

OILY SKIN

You can tell if your skin is oily because it usually has an overall shine. It may be sallow and coarse in texture.

Your skin may be spotty and especially prone to blackheads during adolescence. Oily skin contains a lot of sebum, which helps to prevent the skin from drying out. However, oily skin tends to attract more dirt and dust than a dry skin. It benefits from soap and water, so washing with a cleansing bar is an ideal way of cleaning it.

• Use toners and astringents containing alcohol and always use a light, non-greasy liquid cleanser. Or you could try a two-minute gentle massage, morning and night, with the fingertips, using soap and water or cleanser. But resist the temptation to cleanse your skin more than this.

• Very oily skins need no extra moisturizer, but if your skin is only slightly oily it may benefit from moisturizing the dry areas, such as the cheeks.

• Look out for drier areas such as the lips, throat and the outer parts of the cheeks and forehead; these may need more regular moisturizing.

WHAT KIND OF SKIN IS YOURS?

The colour of your skin is determined by the amount of melanin it contains. This substance protects the skin from the sun's ultraviolet rays.

Fair-skinned (Caucasian)
Your hair is light coloured (or red), your skin is fair (sometimes freckled), and it's always hard for you to get a tan. You tend to burn easily.

Olive-skinned (Mediterranean)
Your skin, hair and eyes are all olive brown or dark brown. You tan quickly and easily, without burning.

Black
Your hair, skin and eyes are black or extremely dark. You don't burn easily.

WHY USE A SUNTAN CREAM?

Suntan creams block the harmful effects of UVA and UVB light. You'll find each cream comes with a sun protection factor (SPF), which equates to the length of time you can stay in the sun without burning.

So if you're sitting in strong sun that would give you sunburn in ten minutes and you apply a suntan cream with an SPF of 10, you can sit in the sun for 10 x 10 minutes without burning. Very pale-skinned people should use creams with the highest SPF or a total sunblock.

SAFE TANNING

All ultraviolet rays in sunlight – both UVA and UVB – are harmful to the skin, and the damage depends on the length of time you stay unprotected in the sun. Long exposure to the sun may inflame your skin and cause it to swell. Even longer exposure results in burning, with blistering and peeling, and possibly heatstroke, which causes the temperature-regulating mechanism of your body to give up, making you very ill.

The most serious danger of suntanning is the risk of skin cancer, which is very high in pale-skinned Northern Europeans. Skin cancer has increased by 40 percent in the last few years and this is almost entirely attributable to our obsession with a tan. Sunblocks are the order of the day. Another long-term hazard is wrinkles, which are caused by the sun destroying the collagen in the skin. A suntan ages your skin and there is nothing you can do to reverse it. Instead, protect your skin with sun cream in strong sunshine. Always wear a peaked or broad-brimmed hat and a protective top and remain "pale and interesting". If you really must get a tan, be sensible and learn all about sun protection factors (see left).

YOUR SKIN TYPE

Knowing your skin type will help you decide how long you can safely expose yourself to the sun without burning (see column, left). If you have a dark skin, you will be able to stay in the sun far longer than someone with pale skin, and you will burn less easily. Remember that if you are unused to the sun, tanning must be done gently and gradually. Start off by staying out in the sun for only a few minutes on the first day, and progressively increase the time as the days go by. You can get just as burnt when you are moving around when say, water-skiing or sailing, as when you lie out on a sunbed. So use your suntan cream lavishly and religiously, and when you've reached your time limit for the day, put your clothes back on. If you are out on water or snow, the strong reflected light will burn you just as much as direct sunlight, and you will need to reapply your sunscreen at least every two hours or so. Take care also if it's very windy because you can still become sunburnt even if it doesn't feel very hot.

MAKE-UP

Except for when going out to parties, you should aim to look as natural as possible and use make-up to enhance your features. Make-up is fun and there are so many inexpensive ranges on the market that you won't have to break the bank to do a little experimenting. Read the magazines to find out what suits your colouring and personality and to discover what goes with your clothes.

Foundation Use foundation cream to cover up any little blemishes and give your skin an even finish. Choose a foundation colour that is as near to your own skin tone as possible. Don't forget to blend it into your neck.

Powder Powder is good for fixing your foundation and it adds a natural bloom to the skin. Loose powder gives an even finish and the surplus is easy to remove, but compressed powder is easier to carry around. It is best to use a translucent one to avoid that orange or pink look.

Blusher Blusher gives your face warmth and modelling. Be careful about where you put it; for example, if you apply it too near to your nose it may draw your face inwards. Sweeping it outwards widens your eyes, and a little under your cheekbones gives you a "chiselled" look.

Highlighter You can use highlighter to give your face shape and to help draw attention to your good points, such as your eyes. It is good for complementing eye make-up – you can put a touch along the top of your cheekbone and under your brow.

Eye make-up For daytime, try to keep your eye make-up as natural-looking as possible. Too much eye make-up can be ageing. Use a light colour to cover your eyelid and eye socket. Next, take a slightly darker colour and shade in above your eye crease and down to the top of your eyelid. If you like it, use a highlighter on your brow bone. Then, outline the eye as close to the lashes as you can and blend in both top and bottom lines so that they don't look too hard. Apply two coats of mascara to upper and lower lashes.

BASIC MAKE-UP

Make sure your face is completely clean before you start. Apply your moisturizer.

1 Dot concealer under the eyes and on any blemished areas, blend in. Apply large dots of foundation to the chin, cheeks and forehead, also blending in.

2 Brush powder all over the face, then apply blusher to the cheek bones, brushing upwards to the temples.

3 Brush eyeshadow onto the lids and then apply a little eye-liner to the outer corner of the upper lid and dot the lower lid. Use a brush to blend in the liner. Put on mascara.

4 Outline the lips with a lip pencil in either the same shade as your lipstick or one shade darker, and fill in with lipstick. Add a lip gloss afterwards if you like.

The finishing touch
Lipstick adds colour to your face and helps to give a finished look.

The vagina is an organ that cleanses itself naturally and it does not need any help from you.

For this reason you should never use internal vaginal sprays or douches even though you may be tempted; they are quite unnecessary and can be harmful. They may contain antiseptics and other chemicals that would disturb the very delicate natural balance of acids, yeasts and bacilli which are necessary for the health of the vagina. You could cause an abnormal vaginal discharge.

You should wash the external genital area frequently, of course, but avoid getting soap and soapy water in the vagina itself. This is because the delicate vaginal skin is easily irritated by soaps, and thrush or candidiasis (a fungal infection) may develop. Some people find that certain bubble baths have the same effect.

PERSONAL HYGIENE

Taking a shower is the best way to get your whole body clean because you are washing under running water. If you don't have a shower and only take baths, stay in the water for the shortest possible time and never soak. This is because soaking and washing remove oils from your skin, leaving it flaky, dry and rough. Use the mildest cleansing agent you can. Soap-free cleansing bars or gels and baby soap are best. Wash underneath the arms with particular care and be careful to rinse because if you leave any soap on the skin it may react with your deodorant and irritate the skin.

Wash your genital area carefully, cleaning the anus separately from the vagina. Make sure that you take the soap from the front to the back and not the other way round, and avoid getting soap and soapy water in the vagina itself (see left).

Dealing with body odours Sweat is part of your body's cooling mechanism. Water on your skin's surface evaporates and helps cool you down. Sweat itself doesn't actually smell; the odour is caused by the action of bacteria releasing rather unpleasant-smelling, but nonetheless natural, chemicals. These also happen to contain chemical attractants for the opposite sex! A deodorant contains chemicals that stop your sweat from smelling, and an antiperspirant limits wetness. If these are applied daily, smells are kept to a minimum.

The underarm area If you have a very strong smell from under the arms, wash as often as you can and change your clothes frequently. You could use a man's unperfumed deodorant, combined with an antiperspirant. It's a good idea to shave your underarm area or use a depilatory cream because underarm hair tends to trap the sweat rather than letting it evaporate quickly. It's better not to apply a deodorant immediately after shaving since your skin surface may be broken and could become inflamed.

Foot deodorants If you are unlucky enough to suffer from sweaty feet, there are foot powders and sprays in the shops that will help keep them fresh. But you will also need to wash your feet frequently and change your socks or tights once or twice a day. Always try to buy leather rather than synthetic shoes and in hot weather opt for sandals rather than trainers.

HAIR REMOVAL

Hair can appear in lots of different places on your body and it's perfectly normal. But if it grows where you don't want it, there are plenty of ways of getting rid of it including depilatory creams, plucking, shaving, electrolysis, waxing and laser treatment. If you prefer, you can bleach your body hair so that it is less noticeable.

The face　You can pluck your eyebrows and the few hairs that grow in between, but you must never pluck or shave hairs on your upper lip or chin, or hairs growing from moles. Electrolysis is the best method in these areas because it's permanent, but it's not really suitable for young girls because your changing hormones may mean that your hairiness is only a temporary phase. This treatment is lengthy and expensive: each hair is individually treated with a needle and it has to be done by a beautician qualified in electrolysis. If you have really excessive facial hair, go to your doctor because you may have a hormone imbalance, which could be corrected by hormone therapy.

Underarms　Shaving is a good way to get rid of underarm hair; you can do it regularly and quickly when you're in the shower or bath. Use plenty of soap and water and rinse well. You can use a depilatory cream for the underarms, too. This is a chemical formula that dissolves the hair. Although this method lasts longer, you may find it a bit messy.

Arms and breasts　Most people don't usually worry about hairy arms; they're accepted as normal. But if you don't like yours, try bleaching them. Nearly everyone has an occasional hair around the nipples, you can pluck them, or snip them with scissors, but never shave them, and never use depilatories or waxes.

Legs　Shaving, waxing and using depilatories are all good ways of dealing with hairs on your legs.

BIKINI LINE

This is a job that is not fun but it just has to be done if you want to wear a swimsuit or bikini in comfort.

Waxing is best for this area; it's painful but the results last a long time. Go to a proper beauty salon to have it done – at least for the first time. Shaving this area can cause skin irritation.

Remember, "perm" is short for "permanent" and although it's not permanent, a perm can take a very long time to grow out.

But if you've decided that a perm is really the answer for you, you should discuss with your hairdresser all the different types of perming that can be done. There are very soft perms for fine, delicate hair, to give the hair body and root lift.

Permed hair gains body, retains curl and style, and is a lot easier to manage yourself. You will be able to make it look good for special occasions without having to rush to the hairdresser.

CARING FOR YOUR HAIR

You can wash your hair every day or every other day as long as you use the mildest shampoo possible and under wash your hair; this means only one application of shampoo, no rubbing or scrubbing, simply leaving it for one minute and then thoroughly rinsing off. No harm will come to your hair. Modern shampoos are very efficient and the manufacturers encourage two washes simply so that you will use more of their product.

Drying your hair It's best for your hair if you allow it to dry naturally. Blowing it dry using a low heat, with or without the help of a brush to give the style shape, is fine, but never blow-dry with a very strong heat because it cracks the hair cuticle and makes the hair more likely to split. If you use heated rollers or hot tongs too much, particularly right to the ends of the hair, the same thing will happen and your hair will look tired and frizzy.

However, hot wands can be a real boon. You can carry them around in your handbag and give your hair a "lift" if you want to look special at short notice. Heated rollers have a longer-lasting effect than hot wands, but they do take several minutes to put into the hair, several minutes to cool, and then it takes a little while longer to comb out and style the hair.

Oily hair Oily hair is a very common teenage problem because your scalp is producing a little more sebum and oil than it should. You can wash your hair as often as you like, but remember to use a mild shampoo and wash only once each time. Avoid using anti-dandruff shampoos, which also stimulate the sebaceous glands to produce more sebum. Try not to brush and comb your hair a lot since both of these activities stimulate the sebaceous glands. You don't need to apply a conditioner with oily hair. If you like, you can also make your hair become drier by having it permed, dyed or tinted, or by using heated hair tongs and wands.

Dry hair If you've got dry hair, your scalp is producing a little less sebum than it should. You should wash it as infrequently as possible – perhaps as little as every four days – and use a mild shampoo. After you've shampooed, use a cream conditioner and leave it on for a few minutes before rinsing. Don't brush your hair out, just comb it gently.

Dandruff Dandruff is not abnormal, nor is it caused by an infection or fungus or whatever shampoo manufacturers would have you believe; you don't need anti-dandruff shampoos. Skin cells are being lost from the surface of your scalp all the time, and the presence of hair doesn't allow the skin scales to drop off. They become piled up into thicker scales which get trapped by the hair, and this is called "dandruff". You can control this kind of dandruff with regular, frequent washing – say every other day – with the mildest shampoo possible. Avoid rubbing or scratching, but make sure that you rinse your hair very thoroughly.

CHOOSING A HAIRSTYLE

If possible, aim for a hairstyle that allows you to wash and leave the hair to dry on its own without too much styling. The best way to find a hairstyle that you like and that's up to date is to flick through a current batch of magazines and notice what styles the models have. Make sure that you choose a style that is realistic for you; compare your face shape with the models' and your type of hair, too. Don't just look at how the hair is cut, notice how it's treated. Is it permed or not? Are curly looks in fashion, or are straight ones? Notice also how the models dress up their hair with scarves, pins, combs and slides. Once you've decided on the style, take the pictures with you to the hairdresser as a guide.

The cut A good cut is the basis for an easy-to-care-for, stylish and interesting hairstyle. Be prepared to tell your hairdresser your likes and dislikes. For example, if you like a certain part of your hair long and would never contemplate having it short, be sure to make this clear. Your hairdresser will probably have ideas for you, so you can work out the cut between you. If you've seen a particular cut in a magazine but you know it's not quite right for you, your hairdresser may be able to adapt it to suit you. Careful cutting can create all sorts of effects, for example, long, heavy hair can be given bounce at the crown by cutting in layers, and it needn't look bitty.

TYPES OF HAIR COLOURANT

Colouring your hair has endless possibilities for achieving many exciting and different effects.

You can opt for a subtle temporary rinse, or use colouring gels yourself at home. You put them on just like shampoo and the colour eventually washes out after several shampoos. Or you can be really daring with permanent multi-coloured streaks. For highlighting, tinting and bleaching, you must go to a professional hairdresser.

• Henna is a natural colourant that will give your hair an overall reddish tint. Its great advantage is that it does not damage the hair, but it can be very messy to use. It has to be kept on the hair for a long time to take effect before washing it out. It's best used on brown hair since the results will be too bright on fair hair and won't show at all on black hair.

• Highlights are a good way of adding interest; they are usually used on fair hair to make it look sun-streaked. Dye is put on selected strands of hair while the rest is left your natural colour.

• Tinting changes the colour of all your hair permanently.

• Bleaching is a strong, permanent way of lightening your hair. It can damage the hair, so you should condition it regularly to keep it looking good. Your roots will show as the hair grows and they will need regular bleaching.

HOW TO GIVE
YOURSELF A
MANICURE

It's well worth taking the trouble to take care of your nails properly. Give yourself a regular manicure once a week and make it part of your beauty routine.

• *Use a fine emery board to shape your nails. Working in one direction only, file from the sides to the centre.*

• *Give your fingertips a good soaking in a bowl of warm soapy water so that the cuticles soften up. Dry the fingers.*

• *With the help of an orange-stick, put cuticle remover around the nails and remove the cuticle or push it down.*

• *Buff the nails with a soft leather buffer from the nail tip down to the cuticle.*

• *Rub hand cream into your hands but make sure that you remove it from the nails, so that you can apply polish if you wish.*

NAILS

Nice-looking nails can really make a difference to your appearance, so it's worth making the effort to look after them properly. It's important to eat a high-protein diet, including foods such as fish, eggs and yogurt, so that your nails grow strong and healthy. It may be difficult to have nice nails if you have to put your hands in water a lot, since water tends to soften nails and they split and tear more easily when they are wet. This can be prevented by wearing rubber gloves for these chores.

Nowadays, if they can afford it, everyone can have long, strong nails with the application of tips, wraps and acrylic, which need minimum care – just a trip to the manicurist every three weeks or so. Even busy, active girls are able to opt for glamorous nails that are much longer than possible just five years ago. If you use a base coat, two coats of polish and a top coat, which you reapply every fourth day, your nail polish won't chip and will stay intact for two weeks or more.

HOW TO STOP BITING YOUR NAILS

Nail-biting is a nervous habit that is very difficult to break, and when it comes down to it, the only person who can do anything about it is you. No-one can stop you from nail-biting unless you really want to yourself, and then it won't be too difficult.

I'm not a believer in putting unpleasant-tasting chemicals on to the nails because it's only too easy to wash them off and start biting again. You must simply find a good enough reason for stopping. For many girls, the appearance of their nails is enough, especially if they have a boyfriend and are embarrassed about their bitten nails.

My own reason for stopping was that I noticed that there wasn't a single nail-biter among the really successful people I knew. That made me determined to stop and I succeeded at the age of 27! One of the things I did to make it easier was to keep my nails as nice as possible, so I gave myself a manicure almost every day. I also found that giving my nails a coat or two of an attractive nail varnish was an added deterrent to biting – I didn't want to ruin their appearance.

"I started to take a pride in my nails and use nail polish. I thought they looked so lovely I couldn't bear to bite them any more."

YOUR EYES

It's important to take good care of your eyes, because no matter how much make-up you put on them, it will be all too obvious if your eyes lack sparkle and are tired. Rest your eyes during the day by simply shutting them and covering them with your hands for a few minutes. If you're at home, you could put cotton wool pads soaked in witchhazel, or fresh slices of cucumber over your eyes for a short time.

Eye tests There isn't any real need to have your eyes tested regularly unless you feel that there is something wrong with them; either that your vision is deteriorating or that you get frequent infections, or that your eyes feel sore and gritty. Visual weaknesses such as short-sightedness, astigmatism or squints can be corrected with glasses from an optician. There's no need to check on the internal pressure of the eye for developing glaucoma until about the age of 40, unless you know it runs in your family. The eyes are not like teeth – they don't need regular check-ups to ensure they're in good health.

Wearing glasses If you do need to wear glasses, they are so attractive these days that they have become fashion accessories in their own right. They're no longer as expensive as they were, now that the provision of frames is outside the monopoly of opticians. You can buy a pair of frames anywhere and have your prescription made up at any optician. After testing your eyes, your optician must give you the prescription for the lenses so that you can go elsewhere if you don't like the selection of frames on offer.

Wearing contact lenses If you don't want to wear glasses you could try contact lenses – many girls prefer them. The safest and healthiest contact lenses to wear are the gas-permeable type because they allow oxygen to reach the eyeball and keep it functioning normally.

There are extended-wear soft contact lenses which can be worn for up to 20 hours, and disposables that you wear and throw away daily. If you are taking the contraceptive pill, contact lenses may not be suitable for you.

CHOOSING GLASSES

When you choose frames, there are several points to think about very carefully before you decide:

- *Do they fit well? Are they resting heavily on the bridge of your nose or is their weight hardly noticeable? Do they slide down your nose? Do they hold your head securely without clenching it too much?*

- *What about the shape? Look at the shape of your face and decide whether the glasses are the right shape for you.*

- *What about the colour? Remember that you're going to be wearing the glasses a lot and they must go with all your clothes. It's best to choose fairly neutral shades: brown, grey, beige or steel rims.*

"I don't like ordinary glasses very much, but I do love those tinted ones because they look so mysterious, so I wear those."

"I've wanted to wear glasses ever since I was a little girl because the frames are so glamorous."

PIERCING

Many girls like to have their ears pierced – it's the fashion – and most earrings in the shops are made for pierced ears. Ear-piercing is unlikely to damage your ears or cause infection provided that you have it done by an accredited person (a doctor, a beautician or a jeweller) and you care for your ears properly afterwards. It is now known that the reuse of ear-piercing equipment could lead to the spread of infections such as hepatitis and even of HIV. Some young people are also having other body parts pierced – such as noses or eyebrows – and the same advice applies.

Think carefully before you have your ears pierced – even though you don't have to wear earrings all the time, the holes are fairly conspicuous, and if you have a change of heart and decide you don't like having pierced ears, you are still left with a scar after the holes have healed.

Look at your ear lobes, are they large or small, fleshy or otherwise? Some people have such minute lobes that there is hardly any space on them for piercing. If you want other parts of your ear pierced, just bear in mind that the holes may take longer to heal and may remain sore and tender for some time afterwards.

Care after piercing After you've had your ears pierced, you must keep the skin meticulously clean. Wash it at least once a day with soap and water and then dab both sides of the lobe with surgical spirit. Keep the holes free of scabs by rotating the earrings frequently (at least twice a day). You must keep the earrings in constantly for at least three weeks until the skin is healed, and you must wear them most of the time for the first year. Newly pierced holes will close up quickly at first, but it will take a period of weeks after that.

You should have gold earrings first of all, and some people find that they are allergic to anything else, but after a few weeks you can usually wear earrings made of other metals. It's best not to wear heavy earrings too often or for long – the lobes can become stretched, particularly as you get older. At school, you'll probably have to wear studs or sleepers to comply with school regulations – in any event, dangling ones can be dangerous if they get caught up accidentally when you're playing sports.

HEALTHY TEETH

A dazzling row of healthy teeth whenever you smile is a must, and the only way to achieve this is to look after your teeth properly and visit the dentist for regular check-ups (about twice a year). Your teeth, and especially the gums, cannot remain healthy if you let plaque build up on the teeth and hard calculus form at the gum margin. These encourage inflammation, which undermines the edge of the gum, so that the teeth eventually become loose. You should brush and floss your teeth at least once a day. Twice a day or after every meal is even better, and your dentist should clean them when you visit, too. Your teeth will benefit from a good diet. Start by cutting sugar and sweet things out of your diet as much as you can, and try to finish off every meal with a glass of water. It's a good idea to chew something raw after every meal, too.

Having your teeth straightened It's perfectly possible to correct misaligned teeth and it's much easier to have it done when you are young than to leave it until you are older. You may need to wear a brace for a while. What braces do is correct teeth by applying pressure very gently over a period of time (a year or so). This persuades the teeth to straighten out by actual movement of the roots in the jaw bones. This should not cause any pain and if there is any discomfort, go back to your orthodontist for a check.

You may be embarrassed about wearing braces, but a lot of teenagers wear braces now. Besides, it's only going to be necessary for a comparatively short time, and the effects will last for the rest of your life, so it's worth it.

Your teeth are important
Take very good care of your teeth because if decay sets in, it will mean more trips to the dentist for fillings and, eventually, extractions.

TIPS WHEN CLEANING YOUR TEETH

When you buy a toothbrush, choose one with medium, round-ended bristles.

1 From the gum margin, brush downwards with a flick of the wrist for the top teeth, and brush upwards for the lower ones, cleaning the front of every tooth.

2 Clean the inner sides of the teeth. Again, brush the top teeth downwards and the bottom teeth upwards, with the same flicking action of the wrist as before.

3 Clean the biting surface of all the teeth, working the brush around and into every crack and crevice. Rinse your mouth out to finish.

4 Use dental floss to keep the gaps between your teeth free from plaque. Wind a good length round the middle finger of each hand and guide it gently down between the teeth to the gum and up again.

BREASTS AND BRAS

When you get to about the age of twelve, your breasts start to develop. Don't try to compare your shape with your friends' and feel that yours are "wrong" in some way; too big, too small, too pointy, or whatever. Just as everyone has differently shaped noses, everyone has differently shaped breasts, too.

It first became fashionable for women to go braless in the sixties. For purely anatomical reasons this fashion spoils the shape of all breasts, except those that are small and light. If your breasts are heavy and you do not support them, the suspensory ligaments stretch. Once this happens, they never return to their original shape and the breasts sag. If you have large breasts, you should help to keep your shape by wearing a bra.

BUYING A BRA

There's no need to wear stiff, heavy bras with under-wiring. Today there are plenty on the market specially designed for girls who lead active lives, who need support, and who want to look as natural as possible. Cotton is the best fabric to choose if you can, particularly if you play a lot of sports. But many good bras are made of synthetic fabrics, too.

For comfort
If you like to be active or are keen on a sport, invest in a sports bra. Made of stretchy materials without added stiffening, it will not ride up and will allow the shoulder blades to move freely.

Measuring for a bra Measure yourself under the bust and round up to the nearest size. For your cup size, measure around the largest part of your breasts and take the first measurement away from this. If the difference is less than 13cm (5in), you are an A cup, less than 15cm (6in) you need a B cup, 15–22cm (7in) a C cup, 23cm (8in) or more, a D cup.

Some major stores offer a fitting service with trained assistants and the chance to try on different kinds and sizes in fitting rooms before you buy. It may be worth doing this to establish what kind of bra suits you.

YOUR FEET AND SHOES

Feet are happiest when they're not wearing shoes at all. This is because your weight is evenly distributed across the whole foot and no particular part takes the strain more than any other. It's obvious that the next best things for your feet are flat shoes, so that the shoeless state is most closely imitated. After that, the higher the heel, the more strain you are putting on your feet, and if you wear really high heels, all your weight will be thrown forward on to your toes. This results in too much pressure being exerted on the front of the foot and you risk developing a bunion (a swelling of the big toe joint).

BUYING SHOES

Have your feet measured carefully first – they may still be growing. Take your time trying on different brands and styles. Don't be talked into buying a pair of shoes if they really don't feel comfortable, some sales assistants can be very persuasive, and they may have their own reasons for wanting to sell a particular pair of shoes. Listen to your feet! And remember that a badly fitting pair won't be worth the misery caused by corns, callouses and blisters – even if they are the latest thing and all your friends have them.

When you try on shoes you should be able to wriggle your toes about and there should be some space between the top of the shoe and your toes. Try on both shoes in the shop and walk around in them. If necessary, close your eyes and think about how they feel. Don't buy ill-fitting shoes and assume that you'll be able to break them in – it's never worth the agony.

How do they look? Think about all the clothes that you will want to wear them with. Will you want to wear them mainly with trousers and jeans, or only with skirts? Will they fit with socks or tights? If they have ankle straps, do they flatter your ankles or make them look fat?

Foot care Don't ignore your feet; they need attention too. If you like wearing sandals, give your feet a pedicure so that they look good. Feet don't need to be done as often as hands; maybe every two or three weeks.

Invest in the right trainers
Sports shoes are expensive so it's important to buy the correct type of trainers for your chosen sport and ensure that they fit you well.

HOW TO TAKE CARE OF YOUR CLOTHES

Your clothes will last a lot longer and look a great deal smarter if you take good care of them from the beginning.

Wash them regularly, but scrutinize the washing labels carefully beforehand so that you don't have any disasters with running colours or shrinkage because you washed them at too high a temperature.

If your clothes have to be dry-cleaned, do it fairly regularly since this will prolong their life. You'll have to wash white items after every wearing so that they keep really fresh. Don't mix coloured clothes in with them – your whites will rapidly turn into greys.

It sometimes pays to soak heavily stained clothes overnight before washing to ensure that the stains come out.

When you handwash sweaters, be sure to dry them out flat so that they retain their shape.

Sports clothes
There's a wide range of fashionable sportswear available now. A tracksuit is warm, comfortable and gives you a sporty image.

YOUR CLOTHES

It makes very good sense to plan your whole wardrobe around one or two classic jackets, skirts and trousers, which are made from good-quality fabric and have very few details on them. You can then wear these with a wide range of different tops. When you are adding clothes and accessories to this "core" wardrobe, try to stick to the same two or three colours that all go together and suit your colouring. Save up for one or two good items and then hunt around in the sales for bargains to go with them. If you like going to jumble sales and second-hand clothes shops, you may find some surprising bargains there, too. It's amazing what some people throw away.

If you enjoy sewing, why not try making your own clothes? These days patterns are designed by top designers and are far from frumpy; you can get easy-to-make styles as well.

Colours This is really a matter of personal preference and will depend on your skin tone, but I suggest that if you are a brunette you could wear combinations of light and dark colours very satisfactorily – say, blue, red, black or grey, and if you are a dark brunette you will look great in dark purples and deep reds teamed with black or white. If you are fair-haired, try the paler end of the colour spectrum; pinks and beiges look good. Redheads can go for the warm autumnal shades such as olive green, russet and shades of brown and use clashing oranges, pinks and reds only for impact.

What style suits you? There's an art in dressing so that your clothes flatter you. For example, if you are shorter than average, you should avoid wearing wide, padded shoulders or loose, baggy sleeves, but go instead for a softer, more flowing line. If you are tall, avoid wearing vertical stripes and opt for a multi-layered look, which breaks up your height. If you are plump, avoid horizontal stripes and fussy patterns; wear plain designs and uncluttered styles, which create longer lines. If you are thin, steer clear of clinging, slinky fabric and choose loose or chunky, textured clothes.

YOUR
SOCIAL LIFE

As much as you love your family, you also need friends –
people of your own age with whom you can have fun
and to whom you can talk about absolutely everything.
Friends are nearly always on your wavelength.
They understand you, share your doubts, dreams
and worries and, most importantly, they love you
for being yourself. But making friends, particularly
with boys, is not always easy to start with. This
chapter gives you tips on ways of meeting people,
advice on how to be a good friend and ideas about
beginning a relationship with a boy.

FINDING NEW FRIENDS

As well as school, there are usually sports centres, youth centres and clubs where you can meet new friends, and it's not a bad idea to see what's going on in your area.

Sometimes you can find out about events by word of mouth from school friends or family, or you could go along to the local library and ask for the names and addresses of local clubs. Most local newspapers carry adverts where you can track down a club for your special interest. Whatever your hobby may be, a club can be an ideal avenue to find other people who enjoy the same hobby.

Friends forever?
Many friendships formed during your early teens come and go but some will last into your adult years.

MAKING FRIENDS

Your teens is a time when you want to make friends. Nearly all teenagers feel that their home life and their family don't give them enough. This is a time when you'll want to broaden your interests, meet people of different types and backgrounds, try out new activities, and belong to a group whose members think, dress and act in the same way as you. Being a teenager is like being a member of a club – you want to stick close to others of your type, who have similar clothes, hairstyles, make-up and also share common values, ideas and interests.

For many of you, friends are your world and it's with them that you want to spend most of your time. In fact, most of each day is spent with friends and, for the first time in your life, parents, relatives and adults tend to take a back seat. You may also be feeling that there is a growing rift between you and your parents and that they do not really understand you, that they cannot possibly see things the way you do, and sometimes that they do not even want to try. Your friends are the people who you feel you want to turn to because they know what you are experiencing and they understand your point of view. They make you feel you belong.

HOW TO MEET NEW FRIENDS

Making the first approach to someone you like in new surroundings can be difficult, but with a hobby or a special interest it's easier because you are doing things together. Sharing a task or learning a new skill gives you plenty to talk about. You'll find it's easy to start up a conversation if you simply make a comment about what another person is doing, especially if it's positive and encouraging, such as "You seem to be getting on all right there," or "You've really managed that quickly". If you see someone who's doing something really well, a good opener is to ask them how they have managed to learn so quickly and whether they could give you a few tips. You'll find that most people are quite eager to show someone else how good they are at a particular skill. It's also easier to make friends during a specific activity because you're all concentrating on doing the same thing; you may even be wearing the same kind of clothes, for instance, if you're going to play tennis or you're swimming, and this acts as a common badge of identity. Or you may have the same equipment, which in itself can be a starting point for a chat. It could be about cameras and lenses if your interest is photography. After all, everyone has a different reason for being attracted to their chosen activity and you can begin a conversation by asking someone why they're interested in it, and then you may find that you have other things in common. What draws people together when they're engaged in the same activity is that they usually meet at the same time of day or week. There may be a lunchtime debating society, an evening chess club or an early Saturday morning swimming lesson, and this regular punctuation of your weekly routine may help to cement a friendship.

BEING A GOOD FRIEND

As with most other things in life, friendship means giving and taking. You'll probably find that if you give a lot to a friendship, you'll get a lot out of it. Conversely, if you give very little, you'll receive very little. Getting pleasure from a friendship is automatic if you work at it, so really you should concentrate on your contribution to a friendship, not on what it gives to you, and the rest will follow. Nonetheless, you'll probably be looking for certain things in a friendship, so it might be a good idea to think about what makes a good friend. Before you do anything else, consider how you behave to see how good a friend you actually are and what adjustments you could make.

BEING PART OF A GROUP

Teenage friendships can be very strong indeed, with bonds so strong that they remain unbroken for the rest of your life. This is partly because teenagers who are seeking to find their own identity and then publicize it, do so by joining groups. The mysteries and mystiques of group identity can form a kind of code that you carry with you for the rest of your life. Friendships within a group also build up deep loyalties and complete trust, which you'll find are very rare in later life.

YOUR GROUP OF FRIENDS

Here are some of the things that can make you feel part of a group:

● *What you wear. Teenagers often wear a "uniform", which is eccentric, often shocking and is certainly different from the "uniform" adults wear. It may be to do with certain garments, for example, a long black skirt. A particular colour or the style of jewellery that you wear may be the badge of your group. Or you may all have a certain type of haircut or a way of doing your eye make-up. Dressed like this you feel you belong, you feel confident, you feel sure of yourself.*

● *How you talk. There are always current word fashions – phrases that make you sound part of the group.*

● *The kind of things you own. It may be a certain kind of school bag, or there may be a craze for a particular type of hi-fi or video, a special game, a cassette recorder or a personal stereo.*

● *What you do. Your group may like to go to a particular sports centre, or going to clubs and dancing, or you may just like sitting around a table in a coffee bar chatting.*

● *Where you spend your time. Certain places, such as a particular record shop or café, may become the province of your group.*

YOUR FRIENDS AND YOUR PARENTS

Don't be surprised if your parents don't automatically take to your friends. They may think that your friends are too noisy, too outrageously dressed, are "up to no good", and are generally having a bad influence on you. Here are a few reasons why:

• Your parents may be feeling hurt because, by choosing friends who are very different from them, you seem to be rejecting their values.

• Now that you have friends of your own, you are obviously growing up and away from your parents and they may be feeling their age.

• Because you're going out a lot, your parents may be a little jealous of all the fun you're having, especially if their own parents were stricter.

• You may be reminding your parents of the good times they had when they were your age.

These are all normal feelings for your parents to have, so try not to get upset and react badly to them. If you can, try to be understanding and open about what you are doing and where you are going with your friends; the more they know, the less they'll imagine and worry about you.

PROBLEMS WITH FRIENDS

There are certain times when friendships can cause you a bit of trouble. It could be because your expectations of your friends are too high. Don't forget that a friendship has to fit into the context of the rest of your life. A friendship may be important, but so are other things, and a friendship certainly shouldn't exclude or threaten other important interests.

BEST FRIENDS AND BOYFRIENDS

You may find that a friendship becomes a bit shaky if you get a boyfriend. Be generous to your friend and encourage her to be generous with you. Don't make her feel that she's not wanted any more. No doubt you'll need each other again in the future, so keep your friendship open and alive. Don't shun your friend, and don't be shunned by her if she gets a boyfriend.

Once one of you gets a boyfriend, you just won't be able to spend as much time together as you previously did, but instead of being secretive about it, or mysterious, just discuss the situation and accept it for what it is. You can't expect to spend as much time together as you once did. It's possible that you won't like your best friend's boyfriend or she may not like yours, and this may put your friendship under a little strain. Only you yourself can decide where your loyalties lie, but be prepared for these tensions to occur. The best possible way is to discuss them with your friend and your boyfriend and keep everything out in the open. It may mean that you lose one of the friendships, but at least you're being honest and realistic about it.

If your girlfriend gets a boyfriend and you don't, you may feel shut out, lonely or inferior. Don't fall into the trap of feeling that you have to compete to get a boyfriend just to stay in with the crowd. You're fine on your own, just as you are.

Occasionally two girlfriends find themselves attracted to the same boy. Between friends it's better not to be devious or jealous. Bring it out into the open and then try to be brave enough to let the third person decide which of you he prefers. If he prefers her, it may take a superhuman effort not to drop your friend because you feel hurt, but try nonetheless.

GETTING TO KNOW BOYS

Before getting to know boys you have to meet them; sometimes it's easy and sometimes it's difficult. Unless you are at an all-girls' school, you will be in daily contact with boys of your own age, and boys who are older, too. Meeting boys at school is certainly easiest because it's part of the normal daily routine, and in mixed classes you are all naturally thrown together. But there are many other opportunities to meet boys, too; for example, social occasions, sporting events, outside activities and part-time jobs. You may also meet them through family and other friends.

It's very unlikely that you'll meet someone and start a relationship straight away, so don't have high expectations of first meetings. Concentrate on being normal and relaxed. Don't ask yourself whether the person is going to turn out to be a friend or someone you love. If you like someone and get on well with them, that's quite enough to start with.

FEELING AWKWARD

All teenagers are awkward at the beginning and starting off a friendship is difficult for everyone. Remember that you are both in the same boat and the other person is probably feeling just as shy as you are. There will be all sorts of questions that you're asking yourself such as: "How can I get to go out with him?"; "What shall we do or where could we go?"; "Should I speak to him?"; "Should I ask for his telephone number?"; "What do I say if he asks me out?" Relax because in all probability he is asking himself almost exactly the same questions.

The first rule when you're talking to someone new is to be yourself: don't put on airs and graces and don't try to make out that you're someone you're not. Act exactly as you feel, not as you think you ought to act. Don't imitate girl-friends who you think have a particularly successful way with boys, it will just seem unnatural and make you even more ill at ease.

Boy meets girl
To help you relax, start by chatting and getting to know each other before you think about whether he is a potential boyfriend.

WHAT BOYS LOOK FOR IN GIRLS

A lot of girls mistakenly feel that most boys who are interested in them are seeking a sexual relationship. But an American survey has shown this to be untrue.

In the survey, when boys were asked "What are the most important qualities that a girl must have for you to want to go out with her?" the following were the ten most frequently mentioned qualities:

1 Good looks and a good body, but not necessarily stunning – "and if she has an awful personality I won't ask her out again".

2 Friendly and not conceited, "a girl who is willing to show that she likes me".

3 Intelligence.

4 A sense of humour.

5 Honest, "doesn't play games or tease".

6 A good conversationalist, "she has to be able to talk to me".

7 Similar interests and values.

8 Sexually candid and frank, "I wouldn't like her to be a prude, but on the other hand I don't want her to have been out with a lot of other boys".

9 Outgoing, not shy.

10 Mature, "I'd like her to have a serious side too".

FEELING GOOD ABOUT YOURSELF

To be yourself you have to like yourself. It's very difficult for anyone to like you if you don't think you're an OK person in the first place. So, if necessary, make a list of your good points and this will give you the confidence to be natural. Don't fall into the trap of thinking that no-one would ever go out with you because you're too boring, too ugly or not clever enough. If you feel like that you'll be nervous, you'll put yourself down and you'll seem and feel unattractive. Just be the person who can chat to the family, crack the odd joke, get on well with strangers, help people if they're hurt or unhappy – and be exactly the same with your boyfriend. Remember that what a boyfriend wants from you is exactly what you'd enjoy in him.

SHOWING HOW YOU FEEL

Once you feel the equal of a boy, you can then show him that you like him and the best way is to give him your attention. A boy can't read your mind. If you're scared and hide your feelings by ignoring him, he's never going to find out how you really feel. So don't be afraid to be the first one to show that you're interested. Of course you'll feel that it's a bit of a risk because you're going out on a limb and there's the possibility that he will show that he doesn't like you. However, it's very rare for someone to be unfriendly to a person who's showing them friendship. A boy is much more likely to respond with a smile than to be hostile and reject you. Remember that everyone likes to be liked and everyone wants to be shown that they're liked. It's always worth the risk, otherwise he's never going to know, and you're going to miss out on friendships in the future.

To get his attention, there are actually some specific things that you can do, such as listen when he talks, look at him when he talks and ask his opinions about everyday things. Without being too obvious, take the opportunity to join in his group and do things with him. Don't be afraid to say when you like something that he does or says. You don't have to sit near him, but smile and occasionally make eye contact. If you pass him in the street say "hello", if you meet him in class or on the sports field, ask him how he's getting on.

Remember when you do give your attention to someone, don't go over the top. Don't try to put on a show, don't try to be the centre of attention, don't be madly witty or try to be the life and soul of the party. Don't over-praise him if it's not justified, for instance, don't say he played the best game of tennis you've ever seen, if it's not true.

Even if people tease you (and they probably will), don't feel a fool. First of all, it's helping your friend to get the message that you like him, it's also helping you to get used to bridging the gap between being strangers and friends. Practice will make it easier, you'll feel more comfortable and you may even get to like it. Remember that if someone doesn't return your feelings, this doesn't mean that you're unattractive. It simply means that they're looking for something else or someone else. It just means that the two of you haven't clicked; don't worry, you will click with somebody else.

GOING OUT WITH BOYS

Having met someone that you really like, the next step is to go out with him. Most teenagers feel less pressure if they go out in a group, and this is how most girls and boys start. It also makes the asking easier and the doing easier if you have a specific activity or occasion in mind.

It doesn't matter at all who does the asking. Traditionally, it's always been thought that a boy should make the first move and for this reason many girls hold back. I think this is wrong. In an honest relationship either the boy or the girl can initiate the relationship. Many boys feel relief that a girl has made the first approach, so don't be shy to do it. Also, a girl shouldn't have to sit and wait.

It's best not to make small talk before you make your move because you may lose your nerve while you're working up to it. Simply come straight out with your suggestion. Of course, you could always write a note; if you do, try to be just as straightforward. There's no need to explain what's behind your invitation; the fact that you're writing a letter means that you must want to get to know him better, and he'll understand that.

It's one step further to ask someone out alone without the rest of the group. Both of you will inevitably get the idea that if you got to know one another you could like

WHAT GIRLS LOOK FOR IN BOYS

According to an American survey (see column, left), the most important qualities that a boy must have for a girl to go out with him are:

1 Intelligence.

2 Good looks and good body but not necessarily handsome.

3 A good conversationalist, "easy to talk to".

4 Sincere and honest, "not just out for sex".

5 Confident but not conceited.

6 Sense of humour and fun to be with.

7 Clean cut, "well groomed, doesn't take drugs or drink alcohol to excess".

8 Romantic and affectionate.

9 Popular at school.

10 Gentle, "doesn't feel that he has to prove that he's a man".

"When I'm with the girls it's all right but when I'm with a boy I'm absolutely tongue-tied, I stutter and just say yes and no. It's so embarrassing."

WHAT ARE BOYFRIENDS FOR?

A relationship should offer many things before you consider having sex together. You may not find everything on the following list but as long as you both enjoy some benefits, the relationship will be a good one. You can give each other:

- *Fun*
- *Company*
- *Trust*
- *Respect*
- *Happiness*
- *Togetherness*
- *Someone to go out with*
- *Someone to laugh with*
- *Someone to cry with*
- *Someone to lean on*
- *Love*
- *Understanding*
- *Support*
- *Sharing*
- *Help with problems*
- *Sharing jokes*
- *Someone to dance with*
- *Someone to talk to*
- *Someone to care for*

each other quite a lot. Sometimes a boy is surprised and unsure of himself when he gets asked out, so don't be too put off if he hesitates and stutters a bit; it may be a few moments before he collects himself together. In his nervousness he may even say "No" in a rather offhand way. If you really believe that he'd like to say "Yes", give him another chance or ask him when he's part of a group.

Most boys and girls these days don't have a lot of money and more often than not "go Dutch", each paying their own share. This is not an embarrassing way of sharing the cost, it's by far the fairest thing to do and girls should be expected to pay their way. To put your boyfriend's mind at ease you might say, and especially if you issue the invitation, something like "We'll each pay for ourselves shall we?" If you say this right at the beginning, neither of you need worry about it later.

FROM FRIEND TO BOYFRIEND

Not all friendships do, or should, go on to become deep friendships. Some relationships are best left as easy, informal, brother-and-sister-type relationships. This doesn't rule out deeper feelings, it simply means that you don't get involved with one another. Involvement brings with it responsibility, so you have to make sure that a deeper, closer relationship is what you really want. Some girls find themselves slipping into a deeper relationship, but others find that they are drawn towards deeper involvement because of what they get out of or put into such friendships.

Most important of all is for you to think about what you have to offer someone else in a relationship, and it's obvious that there are many things you can offer before you even have to start thinking about having sex with him (see column, left). You can make up your own list about yourself and the sort of things you can offer or want from a boyfriend, but try not to get stuck on one idea or image, or you may sit around waiting forever for the right boy to come along. You may not get everything you want immediately; it requires a lot of effort.

RELATIONSHIPS

There are good and bad relationships. A good one usually makes you feel that you're getting what you want and need, yet it's not exclusive, it doesn't block off your involvement in other areas that are important in your life. You'll find that you enjoy the time you spend together and that not all of this time involves being romantic and sexual. A good relationship enables you to enjoy time together with other people, and, almost best of all, it will make you like yourself more and build up your self-esteem. You'll find that you get support, comfort and understanding from him, which is very enriching. In a good relationship such as this, your values may be similar but any differences are exciting rather than upsetting, and you'll find that you can respect each other's views without friction. It could be that your thinking will be stimulated, possibly your creativity too, and possibly you will enjoy the whole of life more – including other people. It's a great comfort to feel security in your partner's feelings for you, and it should be an equal relationship with the two of you making decisions together, or taking turns, so that you find it difficult to say who is boss. If it's a sexual relationship, you'll enjoy making love.

On the other hand, if the relationship isn't going well and you're feeling bad about yourself, it can sometimes help to remind yourself of what your rights are. For instance, if you're feeling embarrassed because of something that you've done or said, it's quite comforting to think that you have the right to make mistakes and learn from them.

You also have the right to be yourself (see column, right). If the the relationship is good, you will have the freedom to do what interests you, such as school work, sports or hobbies and not feel that his friends and interests are more impor- tant. If this is the case, do you really need him?

Feeling unhappy
If your relationship makes you feel bad about yourself, you are probably better off without it.

BEING YOURSELF

Here's a list of your personal rights from **Be Yourself** *by Vicky Wootten, which you might like to take a look at. You'll probably find it reassuring and, of course, you can add any other general "rights" that apply to you as an individual.*

I have the right:
- *To be me*
- *To time with my friends*
- *To time with my family*
- *To make my own decisions*
- *To my own values and opinions*
- *To have respect*
- *To ask questions*
- *To affection*
- *To love*
  - *To support*
    - *To ask for help*
    - *To be depressed sometimes*
    - *To be nervous*
    - *To make mistakes*
    - *To be listened to*
      - *To say what I feel, want, need*
      - *To be silly sometimes*
        - *To show my feelings*
        - *To time on my own*
        - *To be angry*
  - *To say no*

59

WHEN IT'S AN INFATUATION

All of us feel attracted to people, probably many people, throughout our lives, but we don't necessarily need or want to become involved with them.

Many things can attract you about a person, his or her face, smile, appearance, the way he or she talks or moves, and you may feel attracted intellectually, emotionally or sexually. Occasionally, you're attracted to qualities that aren't positive; for example, aggressiveness, or the appearance of not caring.

People find quite different qualities attractive. The most important thing is for you to be sensible about the way you're feeling. If you feel attracted at the level of being friends, then have a friendship and don't pursue it any further. Beware of taking attraction, which is based only on a sexual response, any further without feeling more for that person.

ATTRACTION AND CRUSHES

The subject of first crushes can be of either sex; they can be distant, such as a pop star, or someone quite close, such as a teacher or a boy sitting at the next desk. As well as having a crush on someone of the opposite sex, it's quite common during adolescence for a girl to become very fond of another girl or older woman, and to feel warm and affectionate towards her. This "crush" on a person of the same sex may be your first experience of love. However, the one thing that crushes have in common is that they're usually for somebody with whom you haven't any chance of starting a relationship, and may not even want to. This is possibly because it's the easiest kind of relationship to have; all you have to do is sit and stare at the person or his photograph without having to communicate at all. In other words, you don't have to make any effort and you don't have to take any risks.

LOVE AT A SAFE DISTANCE

It's very pleasant to have a crush on someone because being in love makes you feel good, and it's easiest if you focus your feelings on someone who isn't really part of your everyday life. In a way, you can give yourself up to a satisfying loving or sexual feeling without having to do anything about it or taking on any responsibilities. Sometimes you may go to the trouble of trying to meet the subject of your crush and if they're sensible they'll simply listen, be kind and leave it at that. Sometimes after you've had a crush on someone you get to know them later and then a real relationship can develop – or not; you may find that the real person does not live up to your fantasy about them.

The subject of your adoration can have a profound effect on your life. A smile from the loved one can make you blush and feel blissfully happy, whereas an angry word, a frown or a stern glance can plunge you into despair. The safety of distance, however, allows you to have your first experience of love without the possibility of being injured. Through crushes you can start to find out what love really feels like.

5

ALL ABOUT SEX

Sex in a loving relationship is possibly one of the best,
most life-enhancing experiences you'll ever have.
Unfortunately, sex can also be a minefield, particularly
when you're young. If you're anxious to please, it's easy to
feel pressurized into having sex before you're ready, but this
chapter, with its advice on how to say "no" and the right
time to have sex will help you to sort out your values. You
may be vague about contraception and safe sex and these
subjects are fully explained so that you can protect
yourself. Finally, there is useful advice on how to cope
when things go wrong, with information on such
problems as sexually transmitted diseases, an
unplanned pregnancy and rape.

HOW OLD SHOULD YOU BE?

For all teenagers, this is the million-dollar question. Does age matter anyway you may ask? I think it does for the following reasons.

For purely medical reasons, I'm against very young girls having sex, because as a doctor I know that if you begin sexual activity, especially with several partners, early during your teenage years, it can make you more vulnerable to cancer of the cervix (see p. 84). I am also against any girl having a sexual relationship before she's emotionally mature and has established her sexual feelings and sexual values. For most of us, this is quite a problem and it takes years to sort out; even adults find it difficult.

In addition to these personal issues, I think you would be unwise to ignore the very strong opinions that are held by society in general. Although conventional thinking doesn't matter as much as the opinions of your parents, teachers, friends and relatives, it does matter a bit and you can't ignore it. Everyone has strong opinions about teenage sexuality and you're almost certain to find that your opinions conflict with those of someone who matters to you. Don't ignore this situation completely because your relationship with that person can only deteriorate if you go directly against their views.

THINKING ABOUT SEX

Sex, particularly good sex, is fun and it gives a great deal of pleasure in many contexts. It can be thrilling, exciting, moving, comforting, even consoling. All of these are positive and genuine reasons for having sex. Religious organizations and much public opinion say that teenage sex is immoral, and believe that sex should only take place within marriage. Very often parents pass on a confusing message by teaching morality but holding a fairly liberal view of sexual activities within and outside of marriage. And then there are the questions of safe sex and contraception. Sex is a minefield and you must reflect deeply before stepping on to it.

SORTING OUT YOUR VALUES

Parents should be the first people you turn to when you're trying to sort out your ideas and feelings about sex. For many of the teenagers I've met, however, this is almost impossible.

If you can't speak to your parents, you might try to find an older, friendly, female relative whom you can talk to; a teacher to whom you feel particularly close or an older friend whose advice you respect. Whoever you speak to, talking about sex is important. After interviewing hundreds of teenagers throughout England, I found that all of them felt a great need to talk, but had no-one to talk to. Many felt that talking to someone would be the solution to their problems and the truth of the matter is that talking nearly always helps you to find a solution to everything.

If your parents are approachable and you think you might be able to talk to them about love and sex, then please have a try. Parents are really worth talking to. They've got a lot of experience that helped them to straighten out their own sexual values and you'll probably find that they have some helpful advice to give – even though you may not want to take any notice of all of it. Your parents care for you probably more than anyone else, and they may suggest things you hadn't even thought of.

Unlike some of your friends who you may want to talk to, you can always trust your parents not to gossip. They will treat everything you tell them as confidential. One of the most important effects of your talking to your parents is that it will help them to trust you, reduce conflict on this issue and generally improve your relationship with them.

Even though you may feel you can cope very well on your own without your parents, there's no question that your life and your well-being will be easier and safer if your parents are backing you up.

Many teenagers balk at talking about a difficult subject like sex with their parents, but if it makes it easier, think of it as practising how to communicate with strangers on a difficult subject. This is something that you're going to have to do many times in your life and it's not a bad idea to practise first on your family, where mistakes don't matter too much, and it's also easier to regain good relationships with them.

One last thing, with your parents on your side, you'll actually be stronger and safer. People won't be able to use you or exploit you. You'll have more security and this will make you feel more confident.

It certainly helps if you plan how to go about bringing up the subject of sex. Here are a few tips:
• Most teenagers fall into the trap of assuming that their parents are non-sexual people. You're aware that they must have had sex several times because of the existence of yourself and your brothers and sisters, but it's hard for most youngsters to imagine that their parents' sex life is on-going. Well it is, and you'll have to face up to it. It also means that your parents have built up years of experience on sexual matters and their help and advice could be very useful. They have been through the same experiences that you are going through, so if they're reasonable people it's very unlikely that they won't understand what you've got to say. Most parents, when approached realistically, will try to understand and be helpful.
• Think first about how you'd approach the subject of sex when talking with any other adult. You obviously wouldn't jump in with a question like "When do you think I'm old enough to have sex?" You'd approach the subject much more subtly; so do the same with your parents. One of the best ways of approaching the subject is to ask your mother and father about their early experiences with questions like "Dad, what attracted you to Mum?" If you begin in this way, you can work from

WHEN IS SEX OK?

I have no simple answer as to when you're old enough to have sex. No-one can tell you this. The answer is, when you're able to cope with sexual relationships – and this varies.

You will also find that no two people agree that there's a particular age after which sexual activity is OK. So I'm afraid it's a decision you're going to have to make for yourself, but there are a few things that you should bear in mind.

The first is the law. The law varies on the age of consent (the age under which it is a crime to have sexual intercourse) in different parts of the world, but it usually ranges between the ages of 16 and 18. In the UK, the age of consent is 16, so you would be breaking the law if you were to have sex before your 16th birthday. Personally, I think few people can cope with sex before this age.

Another basic requirement when thinking about having sex for the first time is to make sure that there is absolutely no risk of an unplanned pregnancy. In other words, both of you should investigate, decide on and use a method of contraception with the lowest possible failure rate (see p. 68). Finally, it it vital that you should feel confident that you will not expose yourself to a sexually transmitted disease including AIDS (see p. 80).

the general to the specific, from the experiences of others to yourself, from hypothetical situations to your own.

• While the media, newspapers and advertising provide conflicting messages about sexual values, they're very useful as a starting point for a discussion, so if you're in a group watching a television programme that involves sex or sexual values, start making comments to your parents and asking questions about it. Don't just sit there in an embarrassed silence.

"My mum and dad think I'm an angel and if I tried to talk to them about sex they would think I was dirty, a whore."

• If there is an article in the newspaper that has specific reference to teenagers, such as teenage pregnancies or abortions, you can explore your parents' sexual values and your own by discussing the pros and cons of such a situation. You can also let them know that you're still unclear about your values and you're trying to work them through in your own mind.

• A book like this could help you to open up the subject of sex with your parents. Take a particular subject and ask your parents what they think about it and you'll find out whether their ideas conflict with those that are suggested in the book.

SEX IN A STEADY RELATIONSHIP

The basic foundation for a sexual relationship is having someone who you really care about and respect, and who feels the same about you. Without this, I'm quite certain that you're not ready for a sexual relationship.

No sexual relationship can be a good one unless you both agree that you want to have sex. Hesitate to have a sexual relationship where you suspect your partner is doing it for some ulterior motive. Some teenagers make the mistake of thinking that a sexual relationship will make them feel grown up, or give them the opportunity to get back at their parents, stop them losing face with their friends, or enable them to keep up with the crowd.

It takes some maturity to enter into a sexual relationship and maintain it because you have to have a mature understanding of what your partner's expectations and feelings are. You must also have mutual respect for each other. Sex may be important to you, but it should not mean that you live only for him. Your relationship must allow each of you to do other important things within your lives, separately and together.

LOSING YOUR VIRGINITY

Not all girls are positive about losing their virginity, in fact, more than half have negative feelings. This is not because the loss of virginity as such is bad or painful, it's largely due to the initial programming that some girls undergo as they grow up, that is virginity must be preserved at all costs until marriage. So you may find that your learning and your feelings are in conflict. Almost every girl grows up feeling that her virginity is precious and nearly all girls want to lose it with someone that they care about and love deeply. If they don't, loss of virginity is nearly always an unhappy event. A fairly commonly expressed feeling I came across when talking to teenage girls was this: "I always thought I'd lose my virginity to someone I loved. Later on when I realized I didn't love him I felt really let down."

A similar view was stated very clearly by another girl I interviewed: "I don't really care about my virginity itself, I care about who I lose it to."

Negative feelings about the loss of virginity can also arise because a girl feels she has taken an irrevocable step and in some basic way she will be irretrievably changed. "I felt hurt and scared and sad because it was like losing an important part of me – the little girl in me – and I knew I could never get it back."

Most girls suffer some inner conflict and some outer social conflicts about virginity and have very mixed emotions about it. Sex feels good but it's supposed to be wrong; young girls aren't supposed to be having sex but so many are; what will her friends say if the girl does have sex; what will they say if she doesn't?

It may help you to get the whole subject into perspective if you remember that girls who play sports (and most do during their teenage years) will have lost their hymens anyway during sporting or strenuous activities. This membrane, which guards the vagina, varies in toughness, but

QUESTIONING YOUR SEXUAL VALUES

It's only right that you should have a good idea of your boyfriend's feelings for you and about his sexual values before you decide if you really want to have a sexual relationship with him. Here are a few questions you should be asking him:

- *How do you feel about me?*

- *What does having sex mean to you?*

- *How do you see our relationship developing?*

- *How will having sex change our relationship?*

- *How will my saying "no" change our relationship?*

- *Who will you talk to about it if we do?*

- *What do you plan to do about contraception?*

Are you ready for sex?
Make sure that you have discussed the sex issue together and both really want to have sex before you try it.

WAYS TO SAY "NO"

If you're really concerned about refusing sex, you can try practising some of these statements:

- *No, I hate being forced to do anything.*

- *No, I don't feel ready for it.*

- *No, I'm really too scared.*

- *No, I don't think I know you well enough yet.*

- *No, do you really want to have sex with someone who doesn't want to?*

- *No, I want to have time just being friends, then I can decide if I want to have sex with you.*

- *No, you're hassling me, I'll know when I'm ready.*

- *No, I don't feel I trust you enough yet.*

- *No, I believe I should wait until marriage.*

- *No, I only want to have sex as part of a long-term relationship.*

- *No, not until we've discussed contraception.*

- *No, not until we know there are no risks at all.*

- *No, I don't want to and if you make me that's rape.*

- *No, you're giving the impression you don't really care about me.*

- *No, you're making me think that you'll go off me if I don't.*

- *No, you're moving too fast for me.*

activities such as riding a bicycle, riding a horse, gymnastics or swimming can be sufficient to rupture it early on in life. So the chances are, if you're a sporty person your "virginity" will have been lost without you even knowing about it.

Attitudes towards virginity vary. One girl who was teased about being a virgin said that despite this, "I didn't care, it was really important to me." Another girl believed that staying a virgin until she met the right person was crucial: "I was a virgin until I was 21, which is ridiculous these days but I felt it was important not to lose it to someone I didn't love."

TO HAVE OR NOT TO HAVE SEX

There's only one reason for having sex and that is because you want to. But deciding that you really want to is one of the hardest decisions you'll ever make. You yourself, and nobody else, should decide if you really want to enter into a sexual relationship and only once you have thought everything over, explored your feelings and values, taken into consideration the effect of your behaviour on others, talked it over thoroughly with your boyfriend and disregarded media images and the pressure of your friends. If it's put like that you can see that the decision is not an easy one, nor is it one that should be taken lightly.

There is the other point of view, of course, which says, if it feels good, do it. Some teenagers subscribe to this view, some adults do, too. For them, sex is OK as long as you don't hurt yourself or anyone else. Remember, however, that this is an extremely self-centred view, and could only work if there were no risks attached to sex, and if there were no feelings running deep within society and within the people we know and love. Also, I'm not sure how you can be certain that you or anyone else will not be hurt. You have to be quite mature and experienced before you can judge a situation as complicated as this.

SAYING "NO"

One of the reasons why sex is frightening to a teenage girl is that she's not sure if she will want to go the whole way. She's worried about how she can get out of a situation that she finds is escalating out of control, or which is simply unpleasant. Most girls are worried about how to say no. Most girls know that they can say no but don't know how to go about it. My list of answers (see column, left), suggests how.

There is one basic rule that you must always apply and that is, if you don't feel like sex, don't have it. A few other rules that you might like to follow are: if you don't feel like having sex, don't make excuses, be absolutely honest and say so. Don't say that you have a period, for instance. You also have to make your intentions very clear to your boyfriend. You actually have to say the word "no". That is all you have to say. You don't necessarily need to say more, but it's worth thinking about how you're going to say it, otherwise you may find you have given in because you didn't know how to make your intentions clear. Be persistent. All that's necessary is for you to say no, over and over again.

Afterwards, don't be apologetic about your decision or change your mind and feel as one girl did: "It is so hard to say no and I'm always scared that the fellow will go off me so I end up saying yes. I suppose I haven't got enough confidence in myself."

NOT GOING THE WHOLE WAY

Many teenagers, and many adults for that matter, make the mistake of believing that the inevitable conclusion to sexual arousal is orgasm. The second mistake is that the only way to achieve orgasm is through sexual intercourse. Both ideas are wrong.

For many girls, first sexual experiences don't result in orgasm, indeed, it may take quite a few years for a girl to achieve orgasm during sexual intercourse and for the majority of girls, this doesn't really matter. Girls are much more emotionally involved in lovemaking than boys. The tenderness, closeness and intimacy, the warm loving feelings that sexual activity can bring are quite often enough for a girl and this is true of adult relationships, too. Girls and women in general don't search after orgasms like the holy grail; they see sex in a much wider context and find it more pleasurable for all that.

If you or your boyfriend believes that only through intercourse can you reach orgasm, you should read the information on sex without penetration (see p. 72). You'll find there are several methods of arousal which can be just as exciting as full intercourse.

YOU COUNT, TOO

You can resist all kinds of pressure if you emphasize your own preference, giving a lot of weight to what you actually want. If you feel yourself about to be put under pressure, try a few responses where you stress the "I", such as:

- *There are lots of things I like doing other than sex you know.*

- *I've got to live my own life according to what I want.*

- *I know you've got your values, but I've got mine and mine are more important to me.*

- *It's very easy to have sex, but I want more than that.*

- *An orgasm isn't the be-all and end-all of life.*

- *I'm not behaving like a kid, I'm behaving like an adult; it's childish not to think of the consequences of sex.*

- *I have my own way of doing things, I can't turn myself on and off just to suit you.*

- *Tell me why it's so important to you that I have sex with you.*

GETTING PREGNANT

Whatever stories you have heard, here is a list of situations when you CAN get pregnant:

• *When you are using the withdrawal method (called "being careful").*

• *When you are having your period.*

• *When you are having intercourse for the first time.*

• *When you haven't had an orgasm.*

• *When you have douched (washed your vagina) after intercourse.*

CONTRACEPTION

In any group of girls around the age of 16 or 17 there will be a great many who've had close friendships with boys, a few who are going steady with one boy, and a very few who are "sleeping around". Once you and your boyfriend decide that you want to have full sexual intercourse, it's crucial that you don't have an unplanned pregnancy. If you are thinking of starting a sexual relationship, first make absolutely certain that you want to. Talk over your doubts together and make your own decision. Then, before you start having sex, the most responsible thing to do is to seek advice on contraception.

In the UK, the Family Planning Association, the Marie Stopes Clinic and the Brook Advisory Centre are all groups that are concerned to prevent unwanted pregnancies, and they will give you contraception advice. Doctors, local family planning clinics and teachers are all important sources of help, too.

Your family doctor can always give you contraceptive advice and, as the law stands, a girl under the age of 16 can seek contraceptive advice and receive it without the doctor telling her parents. This is one of the rights of every teenage girl.

PREVENTING PREGNANCY

Pregnancy occurs if a sperm fertilizes an egg (ovum). The usual place for fertilization is in the Fallopian tube, after an egg has been shed by the ovary and is making its way down to the uterine cavity (see p. 12). On average, ovulation takes place on about the 14th day after the first day of your last menstrual period. The journey of the ovum to the uterus can take anything up to 72 hours. Sperm can live up to 48 hours, so it follows that you are fertile for at least five days out of a month. Sex during these five days is quite likely to result in pregnancy unless you are using contraception.

If you don't want to get pregnant, then to prevent fertilization you must use a contraceptive every time you have sex, no matter what time of the month it is. While it's easiest for conception to take place during full sexual intercourse, when sperm are deposited in the vagina, it's by no means the only way. If you decide on withdrawal of the penis before ejaculation (*coitus interruptus*) as your method of contraception, you are running great risks. Before ejaculation, tiny drops of semen escape from the penis and these contain enough sperm to fertilize an ovum.

You should share the responsibility for contraception with your boyfriend. You may decide that you both want to use some form of contraception to minimize the risk. Consider these points before choosing a method: what is the failure rate? What are the side-effects? Is it easy to use? Would I like using it?

The two main methods of contraception are barrier methods and the pill. Less suitable contraceptive methods for a young girl include the IUD (coil), hormone injections and implants.

METHODS OF CONTRACEPTION

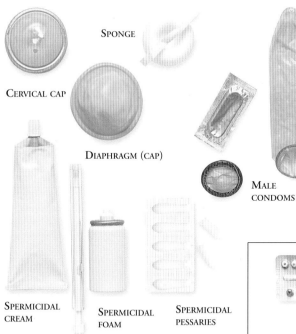

SPONGE

CERVICAL CAP

DIAPHRAGM (CAP)

SPERMICIDAL CREAM

PESSARY APPLICATOR

SPERMICIDAL FOAM

SPERMICIDAL PESSARIES

MALE CONDOMS

FEMALE CONDOM

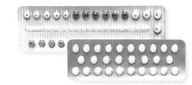

CONTRACEPTIVE PILLS

THE MORNING-AFTER PILL

There is now an emergency pill called the morning-after pill that helps prevent an unwanted pregnancy.

If you had unprotected sexual intercourse at a time when you may be fertile and you are in danger of becoming pregnant, you can take the morning-after pill the next day or during the following few days. This pill makes sure that a period is brought on quickly, which prevents a fertilized egg from becoming implanted in the womb.

Mechanical methods
Condoms (male and female) are available and easy to use; they also prevent the transmission of disease but the failure rate is higher than with the pill. Spermicidal creams, foam or pessaries are used with the diaphragm (cap).

Hormonal methods
The pill and mini-pill are the most effective methods of preventing an unwanted pregnancy. However, some women may experience side-effects. For safe sex, you should also use a condom.

Mechanical (or barrier) methods of contraception These methods stop the sperm reaching the ovum "mechanically" by forming a physical barrier to fertilization. They include the condom or sheath for the male, and the female condom and the diaphragm for the female. Nearly 60 percent of couples in this country use the condom. Both kinds of condom are made of a thin film or latex. The male condom is worn over the penis so that when ejaculation occurs the semen is trapped within the condom and cannot enter the vagina. The female condom is inserted into the vagina before intercourse. Both condoms also help prevent the transmission of diseases such as AIDS.

The diaphragm, or cap, must be placed in the vagina over the cervix, and covered with a spermicidal foam or cream before intercourse to prevent the sperm entering the uterus. You have to go to a doctor or a family planning clinic to be fitted for a diaphragm and you'll be taught how to look after it. The contraceptive sponge, which is impregnated with spermicide, doesn't need to be individually fitted.

Hormonal methods of contraception The other main method of contraception – the pill and mini-pill – relies on female hormones and acts either by preventing ovulation (the combined pill containing very low doses of oestrogen and progestogen); or by making the cervix, the uterine wall and the Fallopian tubes hostile to sperm, thereby preventing conception (the mini-pill or progesterone-only pill); however, the mini-pill's failure rate is lower than with the combined pill.

The pill may have side-effects. Women who are overweight, who smoke and who have high blood pressure are at special risk of thrombosis. If you and your doctor do decide that the pill is the right method of contraception for you to use, then you must make sure that you understand how to use it properly and effectively. You will have to take it every day and at the same time every day, whether you make love or not, for three weeks every month followed by a week's break to allow you to have your period. If you miss a day, to avoid becoming pregnant you must use another method of contraception, such as condoms, for seven days and follow the manufacturer's precautions.

HOW TO USE A MALE CONDOM

The male condom is a barrier method of contraception that is easy to obtain and quick to apply. Putting on a condom need not be embarrassing or inconvenient, especially if you do it together as part of the fun of foreplay.

Some boys prefer it if the girl puts it on the penis. After sex, do not remove the condom until the penis has been withdrawn from the vagina. Check it for any leakage and discard it with care – preferably not down the toilet.

1 Condoms can have a teat at the end, but with or without a teat, first squeeze the end to push out the air so that there is space left for the sperm.

2 When the penis is erect, unroll the condom over the penis to the base. It can be fun to do this together.

3 After the boy has ejaculated, he holds the condom on his penis. Once he withdraws from the vagina, it can be taken off and discarded.

HOW TO USE A FEMALE CONDOM

The female condom is a fairly recent contraceptive device and it is a barrier method that works in exactly the same way as the male condom. It is strong and already lubricated. The advantage of this method is that it allows the girl to take responsibility for safer sex. Like a male condom, it should be used once only and after use, checked for any leakage before discarding it carefully.

To aid insertion, you must squeeze and hold the ring at the closed end on the condom into a narrow oval shape.

Find a position where you can reach the vagina easily and relax to insert the condom

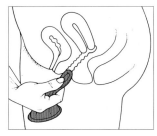

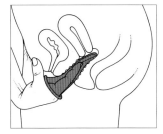

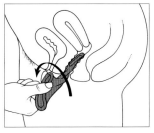

1 Remove the condom from the packaging – it is already lubricated – and with one hand, spread the labia to allow insertion into your vagina. With the other hand, slide the squeezed ring of the condom deeply into your vagina.

2 Then put your finger inside the condom and manoeuvre the ring up as far as you can go. The ring doesn't have to cover the cervix. When it is in place, the condom should hang down about 5cm (2in) outside your vagina.

3 After you've had sex and the boy's penis has been withdrawn, twist the open end of the condom to seal in the sperm. Pull the whole condom out and check it for any leakages before discarding it. Do not use it again.

MASTURBATION

For most of us, our first experience of sex is through masturbation. Masturbation is good for both sexes, it is not wrong and it never does harm unless it becomes an obsessive, frequent occupation.

Masturbation is probably more important to girls than to boys because it's a liberating experience. It allows a girl to explore and experiment with her body long before she will ever have sex with another person. She can stimulate her own body to find out what her responses are and what she likes and prefers.

For all women, the clitoris is the area that is the most sensitive and responsive to stimulation. It's through the clitoris that women are stimulated to reach orgasm. It's nearly always as a result of masturbation that a girl experiences her first orgasm. Some may continue to practise it in a sexual relationship to increase mutual pleasure. Almost all women masturbate at some time – the usual time and place being at night in bed, but it is also common to do it in the bath or in the shower. Many girls just find it comforting to go off to sleep touching the genital area.

Of course sex aids can be used for masturbation. A vibrator can bring you to orgasm quickly and pleasurably and provide a very satisfying means of self-pleasure – something that is every girl's and woman's right.

HAVING SAFE SEX

Safe sex is different from contraception. Contraception prevents pregnancy whereas safe sex stops you getting STDs (sexually transmitted diseases, see p. 80). So if you're going to have sex, to protect yourself you must think about and practise BOTH.

It's easy to get confused about where safe sex and contraception begin and end, because condoms can be used for both. But for young people where pregnancy is a disaster, the failure rate with condoms is too high to make them a reliable way of preventing a baby, so contraception such as the pill is essential. A good arrangement is for you to be taking the pill and for your partner to use a condom.

If you're going to engage in casual sex, something I'd advise you against, mainly because it's associated with cancer of the cervix (see p. 84), again you should be on the pill and you should insist that your partner wears a condom. Or you could opt to take the pill and use a female condom yourself. Insist also that only condoms impregnated with spermicides are used because spermicidal chemicals are potent enough to kill the HIV virus. Remember, spermicides must always be used with any barrier method such as the diaphragm (cap).

Safe sex also means that you must report a suspected STD immediately to an STD clinic where you can get confidential treatment and tell suspected contacts. If you contact a contagious STD such as genital herpes you must always be honest with subsequent partners.

SEX WITHOUT INTERCOURSE

Many adults wish they could recapture the spirit of teenage sexual experience. During the teenage years, having full sexual intercourse is seen as a huge step not easily undertaken. Therefore, foreplay and petting become ends in themselves to a much greater extent than they ever are in adult life. Such sex is more prolonged, more intense than it usually is between adults, and most women regret the passing of the teenage years when foreplay was quite often the only sexual contact they ever got, but it was always exciting and a turn-on. Foreplay is almost invariably satisfying too – which can't always be said for penetrative sex – because it often involves mutual masturbation. This means that the clitoris is stimulated manually or orally, and a girl finds she can reach a climax easily. Often in penetrative sex, where the boy is so eager to penetrate that clitoral stimulation is forgotten, orgasm is difficult and sex is unsatisfactory for the girl.

With adulthood, when sexual intercourse is undertaken more readily, pleasurable, prolonged foreplay is often overlooked or even neglected. This is very sad, but it can lead women to think that teenage sex, though not always as fulfilling, was possibly the most exciting sex they ever experienced. So, I feel it's very good advice to teenagers to enjoy as much as possible a sexual relationship without full sexual intercourse. It's more exciting than it may ever be again, it's safe and it's possible that it will be overlooked as you grow older.

FOREPLAY

In a good sexual relationship there are masses of things to do other than the act of sexual intercourse. Think of sex as being the proverbial iceberg, with sexual intercourse being the visible tip – the one-eighth that is showing above the surface – and all the foreplay, kissing and cuddling being the seven-eighths that are underneath the surface. Here are some of the activities that make up that hidden seven-eighths:

Touching Between people who are attracted to each other touching, even the brushing of fingertips, is intensely pleasurable. Touching can extend to stroking, gently scratching, rubbing, massaging and tickling the whole body, including the hands, arms, face, neck, ears, shoulders, torso, breasts, thighs and genital area.

Kissing This is not the kind of kissing that one does when meeting or saying goodbye to friends. This is long, deep kissing, deeply felt, exploring the mouth and other parts of the body with your tongues.

Nibbling, biting and licking These are natural extensions of kissing; so are nuzzling, nudging and rubbing with the face, over any part of the body where it feels pleasurable and fun.

Petting Touching the breasts, nipples and genitals usually starts gently and slowly so that you can respond to what seems pleasurable to each other. It helps if you talk to each other, saying if something feels nice and asking if something feels good.

SEXUAL AROUSAL

Sexual arousal happens all over the body. As a woman becomes sexually excited, her heartbeat increases so the pulse becomes rapid, the breathing becomes faster and she feels hot and may sweat. The skin will usually become flushed and even have a blotchy look. This is absolutely normal and is one of the first stages of arousal.

Blood flow increases to all parts of the body, but particularly to the genital organs and this is why the breasts become tenser, the nipples become erect and the areola around the breasts become a dark-pink colour. All parts of the genital area swell; the labia and the clitoris increase in size and the vagina starts to secrete mucus for lubrication so that penetration is more comfortable.

At the same time, a great deal of excitement is felt, such as butterflies in the tummy, a warm sensation in the genital area; some women say that tingling in this area may be such that it feels like an actual ache. Various muscles in the body start to tense up, especially in the thighs and legs and at orgasm muscle tension can make the legs stiff. This is perfectly normal.

In boys and men, the main effect of increased blood circulation to the genital organs is an erect penis, but other organs are affected, too, including the testes and the scrotal skin, which becomes very sensitive.

BEING A LESBIAN

Every woman should have the right to choose who and how she loves. Most women opt for a heterosexual lifestyle, some accept a heterosexual lifestyle but continue to have important and loving relationships with women. Other women choose a lesbian lifestyle. A lesbian is a woman who loves women. Lesbian relationships are those in which women share joy and sexual fulfilment. Lesbianism is as natural, though not as common, as heterosexuality. Lesbians are not in any way biologically different from other women, nor do they, as some people suggest, have different family backgrounds from heterosexual women.

"I felt so lonely and different that I went along to the Citizen's Advice Bureau and they gave me a couple of addresses of women's groups and I've met lots of people since then."

Many lesbians go back over their childhoods trying to find early symptoms or causes of lesbianism such as having lesbian dreams or crushes on older girls or female teachers, or experiencing an orgasm with another girl at an early age, but this is rationalization, there's no science in it.

Being a lesbian is about how you want to live your life, including finding sexual and emotional fulfilment with another woman. Sex between women can be intense, passionate and loving, but just like heterosexual love it can also be disappointing and destructive. There are many myths about sex between women, for example, lesbians are often represented as sexual superwomen. Some people also transfer their ideas of heterosexual sex to a lesbian relationship, thinking that one woman must play the part of the man and the other the woman.

"People think that lesbians are sex mad. We're not. We just like women more than men and want to stay with them. How can that be abnormal?"

Lesbianism is more a choice of lifestyle than a sexual choice. Lesbian relationships are less based on sex than heterosexual ones — they're more to do with the desire to relate to women, to live with and to love women. If you suspect that you are drawn towards lesbianism and may be a lesbian yourself, how will you know? According to most lesbians, you will know simply because the truth will come out.

When you first discover this, you may feel very isolated, but you can meet other lesbians by contacting a lesbian befriending service or going along to a lesbian group. Contact numbers are in newspapers and books about sex.

SEXUAL INTERCOURSE

After foreplay, when both partners are ready, that is when the vagina is wet and the male partner has an erection, the penis can be guided into the vagina. Once the penis is in the vagina, either partner can move up and down, backwards and forwards, or from side to side so that the penis is held or rubbed by the sides of the vagina. It's up to the individuals as to what kind of strokes are used – long and slow or short and fast. A woman is usually brought to orgasm by stimulation of the clitoris indirectly by the penis. Rhythmic penetration of the penis can pull on the skin around the vagina, thence on the clitoris and a woman can achieve orgasm that way. This is by no means enough for every woman and quite often either she or her partner will have to rub the clitoris to achieve orgasm during intercourse.

Orgasm is brought about in men by friction of the vaginal walls and vaginal muscles on the penis. Orgasm is much the same between sexes, except that men ejaculate semen. Unlike women, male orgasm is usually inevitable.

WHAT IS AN ORGASM?

It's not easy to put the sensation of an orgasm into words, because it's different for everyone. Before an orgasm you become increasingly excited, breathing is more rapid, the heart beats more quickly, the lips become a darker pink, the pupils of the eyes dilate, the nipples become erect and the clitoris swells and becomes erect and exposed. With more excitement, all of the skin becomes flushed, it begins to sweat and the breasts become enlarged as they are engorged with blood. The labia, clitoris, vagina and pelvic organs enlarge in very much the same way as the aroused penis enlarges and becomes erect. Sometimes there is a plateau of excitement, which is held for several minutes, when you are on the brink of orgasm.

The orgasm happens when excitement seems to go over the brink – a crescendo or climax is reached, which may last several seconds. During orgasm, the body stiffens, the muscles contract and sometimes you may scream. Then the muscles of the vagina relax and contract rapidly, as do the muscles of the uterus. The glands of the vagina discharge a watery secretion, which is the female equivalent of ejaculation.

HOW TO TELL IF YOU'RE PREGNANT

If you think that there's a chance you might be pregnant, here is a list of symptoms to look for:

- *A missed period, if your periods are usually regular.*

- *A short, scanty period.*

- *Swollen, tingling breasts and darkened nipples.*

- *Wanting to pass urine more often than usual.*

- *More vaginal discharge than you usually have.*

- *A strange taste in your mouth.*

- *Feeling more tired than usual.*

- *Suddenly going off some foods.*

If you have any or all of these symptoms, go straight to a doctor or a family planning clinic and ask for a pregnancy test. You will need to take along a small sample of your urine, preferably an early-morning sample. If you don't want to go to a doctor or clinic yet, you can buy a do-it-yourself pregnancy testing kit from any chemist and get a result very quickly. However, these are expensive.

IF YOU'RE PREGNANT

Once you have begun a sexual relationship, even if you use some form of contraception, there is always a chance of you becoming pregnant. If you think you may be pregnant (see column, left), it is important to have your pregnancy confirmed by a test as soon as possible.

If you do become pregnant, the best, though the hardest, thing to do, is to tell your parents as soon as possible. You wouldn't be the first girl to feel that you cannot tell your parents out of fear or because you don't want to disappoint or shock them, but they will find out eventually and it is better for them to find out from you. Don't do what a lot of girls feel forced to do and keep the news of your pregnancy secret. Don't carry on at school for as long as possible because in the later stages of pregnancy certain school activities such as gymnastics are dangerous.

WHAT TO DO NEXT

Every girl has thought about the fear and dread of confessing to her parents that she's pregnant, even if it was only in her imagination. Contrary to what you may think, after the initial shock, most parents respond to this news very positively. Conscious of the anguish that you must be suffering, they'll be aware that you need help, support and counsel and, as they love you, they'll want to be the first to give those things. If they believe that getting pregnant is a cause for punishment, many of them nonetheless will realize that the worry and anxiety that pregnancy is causing you is punishment enough, so take your courage in both hands and tell them. If you have an ally in one parent, tell him or her first and ask that one to tell the other. To give you moral support, it can also help if you tell a sympathetic close relative and take this person along with you.

Don't tell your parents without preparation; try to work out what you are going to say. Also try to make up your mind to a certain extent about which of the options (see column, right) you wish to take. If you know that you want to have an abortion, you must tell your parents and seek help as soon as possible after you have confirmation that you're pregnant because by law there is a time limit within which it has to be done (see p. 79).

You will probably find that your parents aren't at all keen to force any decision on you and will probably be grateful if you have decided on a particular line of action. In the end, they are concerned for you and will really only want you to do what you feel you will be happy with. Then you'll probably find that they'll become much better friends than you ever thought they could be.

TELLING YOUR DOCTOR

It's dangerous to keep a pregnancy secret because all pregnant women, and particularly young girls, need very careful antenatal care as soon as possible. The sooner your pregnancy is being looked after by a doctor the better, so even if you cannot face your parents, you should go along to your doctor.

For many girls this isn't a very attractive alternative because they feel they do not know their doctors well enough and are embarrassed to talk to someone who is a comparative stranger. If this is the case, you should go to one of the agencies that gives advice to unmarried mothers. Please do this as soon as you suspect you are pregnant (that is if your period is more than two weeks late) because you need medical attention, counselling and a lot of support to help you cope with your anxieties, your decisions and, if you decide to go ahead and have it, your pregnancy and the baby.

DECIDING WHAT TO DO

No-one can advise a girl what to do about her pregnancy – you have to come to that decision through soul-searching and lots of discussion with your boyfriend (if he's still around) and with those adults you can take into your confidence. I believe that all girls should know what options there are so that they can then make an informed, considered decision as to what is best for them. In the end, however, you're not going to be able to take anybody else's advice; you will have to weigh up your future and your ambitions, look at your strengths and your weaknesses, think about your maternal drive, as well as your career potential and then make a decision that is right for you. Don't allow yourself to be forced into a decision that you're unhappy with just because it's the easiest answer for other people. You will live to regret any decision made for that kind of reason.

WHAT ARE YOUR OPTIONS?

Having done quite a bit of research into this issue, by visiting centres for teenage mothers in the US and talking to many of the girls there, I realize that any of these options can seem attractive to a girl who is pregnant. It's therefore impossible, nor would it be right, for me to advise what course you should take. Your options are:

- *Marry the father and have the baby.*

- *Don't marry the father, though you could live with him and bring up the baby.*

- *Decide to go through with the pregnancy and bring up the child on your own as a single parent.*

- *Have the baby, but have it fostered or adopted.*

- *Have the baby, continue to live with your parents and perhaps they can look after the baby while you study or work.*

- *Have an abortion.*

I've heard girls say with certainty and joy that the only way they could foresee a chance of future happiness was to have the baby, but have it adopted. I've heard other girls say with utter conviction that they couldn't possibly carry a baby and then give it away – they want to keep the child at all costs. For others, the idea of adoption or fostering for their child is unacceptable and the only way out is an abortion.

HAVING AN ABORTION

If you should decide on an abortion, you should arrange it as soon as possible because the earlier it is done the safer it is. The later you leave it, the greater the chances are of complications. No doctor likes to perform an abortion after twelve weeks, although abortion is legal up to the 24th week of pregnancy.

In the UK, before you can have an abortion, by law two doctors must testify that they feel that the continuation of the pregnancy would be damaging to your physical or mental health, or that there is substantial risk that the child will be born seriously deformed or with a life-threatening disorder. If you and everyone concerned are in favour of an abortion, then you must consult your family doctor as soon as the decision is made. He or she can then direct you to specialists who will perform the abortion.

"I wasn't too upset until I'd had the abortion and then afterwards I just started crying all the time. I suppose it had more effect on me than I thought."

If you cannot tell adults and you feel you cannot go to a doctor, don't ever contemplate having an illegal abortion because they're dangerous and quite unnecessary since, if you really need an abortion, you can get one legally, even if you have to pay. As a last resort, you can always go to a clinic that specializes in giving confidential advice to pregnant women on their own, and it will put you in touch with a team of people who will see that you get your abortion by legal and medically safe means.

FEELINGS ABOUT ABORTION

Quite a lot of girls feel that it is morally, religiously and biologically wrong to interfere with a pregnancy in any way and are therefore opposed to abortion. Others are just as fervently in favour of it. But many of us are somewhere in between and suffer an agonizing mixture of feelings if an unwanted pregnancy occurs.

"I hated the idea of taking an unborn baby's life but I had to do it. It's had the most enormous effect on me and I don't think I ever want to become pregnant again."

We may be afraid of what will happen when our families, relatives and friends find out and we think we will be punished. We are afraid that we won't be able to decide what to do at all and this indecision adds to our anxiety. We are afraid that we will be rejected and alone, that our boyfriend won't stick by us, and of course we are afraid of having to bring up a child on our own. All of these fears are perfectly normal. No girl has an abortion without being psychologically affected to some extent and you may suffer minor depression afterwards. So be prepared to feel withdrawn, depressed, tearful, inadequate and not able to cope well or to take decisions. However, the majority of girls feel relieved after having an abortion, as well as a bit sad.

You are going to have a fairly hard time and you need support, so make sure that you have a friend or family member who will stand by you during and after the abortion. Make sure that he or she can stay with you, take you home afterwards, and stay with you at home, too. You may find one of your parents is a tower of strength, and you can always talk to your doctor if there is no-one who can help you.

AFTER YOUR ABORTION

- For the rest of the day take things very easy and don't take any strenuous exercise for at least three days.
- If you bleed heavily, vomit, have a fever, smelly vaginal discharge or severe pain, contact your doctor straight away.
- On about the third day afterwards you may get a slightly heavier blood flow and cramp pains. If these persist, see your doctor.
- Do not use tampons for two or three weeks or for your first period afterwards. Use pads instead.
- Have a medical check-up six weeks after having the abortion, even if you are feeling quite all right.
- Abstain from sexual intercourse while you still have bleeding after the abortion (this should be a few days).
- Start using some form of reliable contraception.

METHODS OF ABORTION

Some methods and their time limits are:
- Vacuum, or suction, abortion (4–8 weeks of pregnancy).
- ERPC (or D & C) where the cervix is dilated and the pregnancy is evacuated from the uterus under a general anaesthetic or epidural (4–14 weeks of pregnancy).
- Induced labour termination in which prostaglandins are given to induce premature labour (15–24 weeks of pregnancy).
- Hysterotomy – a rarely used major operation in which the fetus is removed through incisions in the abdominal wall and uterus (16–24 weeks of pregnancy).

SEXUALLY TRANSMITTED DISEASES

By far the majority of people decide to have one lover at a time. A few decide to have several at the same time, and if they do, they are behaving in a way that some people would call promiscuous. This may be your choice, but there are certain issues you should consider because, quite beside any moral and religious judgement of what is right and wrong, there are problems and quite a few risks attached to having sex with more than one person.

THE RISKS OF PROMISCUITY

• The chances that you could catch a sexually transmitted disease (STD) and the risks of you developing cancer of the cervix are greatly increased.

• If you or your boyfriend have had other partners, there is a risk of contracting HIV, leading to AIDS. It is therefore crucial for all young couples to use condoms and spermicides every time they have intercourse to reduce the risk, regardless of whatever other contraceptive they are using.

• By squandering time and emotional energy on more than one relationship you may find that you don't have enough time or energy to make any one of them work.

• You are greatly increasing the risk of hurting other people who don't approve of what you're doing.

• You may not think so at the time, but you are running the risk of losing your self-respect if you have even a tiny suspicion that what you're doing isn't right.

• People who disagree with your values are quite likely to label you, and you may get a bad reputation.

TYPES OF DISEASE

While sex is one of the ways of showing affection, it is also a way of spreading certain diseases. The labels "venereal disease" and "sexually transmitted disease" (STD) are now synonymous. There are quite a few sexually transmitted diseases, most of which are very unpleasant, some of which are incurable. They are nearly always infectious and are contracted only by having sex with another person. Here are some of them:

• Genital warts and genital herpes are viral infections;

warts are curable, herpes is not, but the symptoms can be treated. The warts virus can also lead to cervical cancer.
• Gonorrhoea, syphilis and chlamydia are bacterial infections, which are treatable with antibiotics. However, chlamydia is difficult to diagnose as it's often symptomless. It can also cause pelvic inflammatory disease (PID).
• HIV/AIDS and hepatitis B are incurable viral infections; AIDS is fatal, although hepatitis B is not.
• Pubic lice ("crabs") and scabies are parasites, which are treatable with insecticides.
• Candidiasis ("thrush") is a yeast infection, which is treatable with a fungicide.
• Trichomonas is a single-cell parasite, which is treatable with anti-parasitic agents.

HOW TO TELL IF YOU HAVE AN STD

Some STDs are symptomless in the early stages or have very vague symptoms, but if you have any suspicion about having contracted an STD and have any or all of the following symptoms, you should seek medical advice immediately:
• Pain when passing urine or moving your bowels.
• A smelly, discoloured vaginal discharge that is greater in quantity and odour than usual.
• Any vaginal discharge accompanied by a rash or that makes you sore and itchy.
• Lower back pain or pain in the pelvis or in the groin.
• Pain when having sex.
• A sore lump or spot on any part of the genital area, including around the anus.
• A fever, combined with any of these symptoms.
• Oral sex may lead to symptoms around the mouth, including a sore throat.
• Anal sex may result in symptoms around the anus.

Where to get help Most people who think that they've got an STD are too embarrassed to visit their own doctor. This need not cause you any delay. There are special clinics – called STD or GUM (genito-urinary medicine) clinics – in every major city that are well advertised and guarantee confidential treatment. If you want to find the clinic nearest to you, ask at your local advice or health centre, ring up the hospital or look in your phone book. In the UK, these clinics are free.

TAKE IMMEDIATE ACTION

There are certain steps that you should take immediately if you suspect that you have an STD:

• *Find out and visit the nearest STD or GUM clinic.*

• *Stop having sex altogether.*

• *Tell your partner or partners, past and present, about the possibility of infection. It's embarrassing, but they may have had it without knowing. It's important that you tell your partners because they may reinfect you and they may reinfect others.*

• *Ask your partners to track down the person they think they caught it from. It's essential to trace all contacts – it's the only way to stop the disease spreading further.*

IF YOUR PARTNER HAS AN STD

The only really sure way of knowing if your partner has an STD is for him to say so. He's unlikely to volunteer this information, so you're going to have to ask. This isn't easy because your emotions may run away with you and you may forget to ask. It's probably the last thing you want to do when you're feeling passionate. However, STDs are widespread at the moment, and HIV is too dangerous to ignore, so my advice would be never to have unprotected sexual intercourse casually with someone you don't know very well and particularly if you cannot therefore ask this question in a serious or, alternatively, a jokey way.

There are some telltale signs of an STD but they're not obvious and in the excitement of the moment you wouldn't even notice them anyway, even if you could see them. Gonorrhoea, for instance, causes a pus-like discharge from the penis or the vagina, but it's not always obvious in women. Herpes has no telltale signs whatsoever unless it's active with blisters, and HIV can be "silent" for years.

If you want to avoid an STD, you only have four options:

• Remain celibate.

• Practise safe sex – always use condoms with spermicides (see p. 69).

• Only have one sexual partner at a time.

• Insist that your partner has only one sexual partner, and that is you.

Certain STDs, such as chlamydia, can cause pelvic inflammatory disease with subsequent infertility if they're not treated promptly and adequately. This makes it very important that you seek help on the merest suspicion of having an STD.

AIDS/HIV

AIDS (Acquired Immune Deficiency Syndrome) is, as its name suggests, a deficiency of the body's immune system, which means that the body loses its ability to fight a variety of infections and cancers. It is the final and fatal stage that results from infection with a virus called Human Immunodeficiency Virus (HIV). HIV is the most dangerous of all the STDs because at the moment there are no vaccines or cures, although treatments have been developed that slow down the effects of the virus.

HIV isn't a virus that picks on certain types of people; because of the ways that it can be transmitted, men and women are both at risk, whether they are gay or straight. Although initially HIV was found mainly among gay men, the number of cases being passed between heterosexuals is increasing worldwide.

HIV is transmitted through body fluids, mainly semen and blood, but also through vaginal fluids and breast milk. Getting HIV has nothing to do with who you are – but it has a lot to do with what you do. You owe it to yourself and your partner not to be complacent.

Infection happens in five main ways:
• Sexual intercourse with an infected person.
• High-risk sex, in particular anal sex, with an infected person.
• Sharing needles and other paraphernalia for injecting drugs with an infected person.
• Infected blood or blood products given in blood transfusions or other treatments. (This is rare in the UK nowadays because donated blood is always screened for HIV infection.)
• About 1 in 4 HIV-positive mothers may infect their babies either in the womb (the virus passes through the placenta to the baby) or while giving birth or breastfeeding.

Testing for HIV The virus takes from about three to six months to be detectable in the body. People who are found to have the virus are said to be "HIV positive" because they have developed antibodies to the virus that can be detected "positively" in a blood test. (Antibodies are substances produced by the body to fight off infection by a particular virus.)

How the disease develops It can take ten years or more for an HIV-positive person to develop full-blown AIDS. However, once you're infected, it seems that the development of AIDS is inevitable at some time, and the eventual breakdown of the immune system means that a person with AIDS is fatally vulnerable to diseases that healthy people rarely succumb to.

PROTECT YOURSELF

Since it's not always possible to know with whom your partner has been having sex, it is very important for you to take precautions to protect yourself at all times:

• *Never have unprotected sex: always use a condom and spermicides, which actually kill the virus.*

• *If you are an injecting drug-user, you should never share equipment.*

• *If you decide to get a tattoo or get your body pierced, make sure it's done with sterile equipment by a reputable person.*

HAVING A SMEAR TEST

You shouldn't be menstruating or have had sexual intercourse within 24 hours of having your test because blood and semen make the results unreliable.

1 A warmed speculum is passed into the vagina to separate the walls so that the doctor can see the condition of your cervix.

2 A wooden spatula is wiped across the cervix, and the smear is transferred to a glass slide and sent to a laboratory for analysis.

3 The results should be available within six weeks.

HOW OFTEN?

The major debate at present is how often women should be screened for cancer (some say two years, others five) and how fast the results are received. The test is simple and quick, but the system depends on the efficiency of procedures notifying women of their results and when their next smear test is due.

CERVICAL SMEAR TESTS

Cervical smear tests are particularly important for girls who start having sex in their early teens because the young cervix seems vulnerable to cancerous changes when exposed to semen early in fertile life. Cancerous change is even more likely if you have several partners. Promiscuous sex also increases the chance of being infected with genital warts, the virus that also promotes cervical cancers.

WHAT THE RESULTS MEAN

The results of a smear test are classified into several categories:
- Negative: A negative result gives you the all-clear.
- Mild dysplasia (CIN I): This means that you have some infection and should be screened in six months.
- Moderate or severe dysplasia (CIN II and III): Though not always indicating cancer, this means there is a change in cells that requires further investigation.

With mild dysplasia, you'll probably be required to have a regular smear test every six months. With moderate dysplasia you may have to have a colposcopy. With this, the colposcope (a sort of microscope) is placed at the entrance of your vagina to give a magnified view of the suspect area, and cells are removed for laboratory tests.

The next step is a cone biopsy, which allows for a further small number of cells to be examined. The entire layer of suspect cells is removed with a scalpel or laser beam under general anaesthetic. If cancerous cells are discovered, treatment is given for cervical cancer.

THE SMEAR TEST RESULTS

Result	What action is taken
Negative	No follow-up needed. Next test in 2–3 years
The mildest inflammation, known as mild dysplasia (what doctors call CIN I)	Another smear test in 6 months
More severe inflammation, called moderate dysplasia (CIN II)	Colposcopy
Severe dysplasia, with or without invasive cancer (CIN III)	Colposcopy with or without cone biopsy

RAPE

The rape of women and children is becoming more and more common, although it is estimated that between 75 and 90 percent go unreported. One of the reasons that makes it difficult for girls and women to report rape is that it often occurs between people who know each other, making it hard for the woman to prove that it has taken place. Rape may occur in circumstances in which the victim feels that she is not able to tell anyone, or that she is not likely to be believed. Rape can also take place when women find themselves in compromising situations, such as when they are hitch-hiking or out alone. Sometimes rape victims are not keen to report the incident because they feel that the police and the courts will not be sympathetic. Recently, a great deal of work has been done to change this attitude. There are now many rape centres, run both by the police and by ordinary women, where there is no insensitivity, callousness, obstructiveness or disbelief, and victims are treated kindly and sympathetically and are given all the support that they need.

IF YOU ARE ATTACKED

If you find yourself in a situation where you're being sexually assaulted, scream as loudly as you can and fight. Try to get a finger in the man's eye, or pull your knee up into his groin.

You're going to have to judge things rather carefully. If your assailant is armed, lack of resistance on your part may be necessary to save your life. If you decide that resistance is useless or is likely to lead to greater violence do the following:

- Stay calm, talk quietly, remind your attacker that you're human.
- Answer leading questions about your feelings with something factual like "You're hurting my back".
- Concentrate on the rapist's identifying features and clothes, any regional accent or speech patterns, birthmark, tattoos and jewellery.
- Think about how you'll notify the authorities once you are free.
- Try not to show any pain because it might make the rapist more violent.

HOW TO AVOID RAPE — ON THE STREETS

When out alone at night take a few basic precautions:

- *Avoid walking alone on the streets at night – take a taxi.*
- *If you have to go out alone at night, don't venture into areas where you know there has been trouble.*
- *Avoid streets that are badly lit, narrow alleyways, areas of desolate wasteland or woods.*
- *If you feel that you're being followed by a man who you fear may attack you, run into the middle of the street and start screaming. Or run to the nearest lit house, knock on the door and ask for help.*
- *Carry an alarm in your handbag.*

HOW TO AVOID RAPE — AT HOME

You should be safe at home as long as you don't allow strangers or unwelcome visitors in. Make sure you:

- *Have strong locks on your windows and doors.*
- *Install and use a peephole.*
- *Put a safety chain on your door, and use it.*
- *Never open your door to a man who says he has come to do a job without seeing his proof of identity first.*

TELLING A FRIEND

If you have been raped, you may need a friend to talk to and preferably stay with you for a few days afterwards.

When you ask someone to stay with you, choose a friend who really cares for you rather than about the fact that you have been raped. Many people have conflicting ideas about rape and they may want to concentrate more on it rather than on you. This will not help you at all. If you can, go along as soon as possible to a rape crisis centre – especially if you don't feel you can contact the police on your own. The people there will understand all that you have been through and be sympathetic and comforting. They will seek legal advice on your behalf and help you get through this difficult time in every way they can.

AFTER A RAPE

If you have been raped you should do these things:
● Telephone a friend or relative who can get to you quickly.
● Ask them to stay with you at all times for the next few hours.
● You or a friend should report the crime to the police.
● See your doctor or go to a hospital as soon as possible.
● Do not take a bath or wash yourself. Put your clothing in a plastic bag and don't wash it. Take it to the doctor and police for examination.
● Write down everything you can remember and any identifying features of the man.
● Don't go home alone from the doctor's or the police station. Get a friend to stay with you that night or go and stay with friends or relatives.
● Contact your local rape crisis centre as soon as possible.

You will also find it helpful to contact a local victim support organization, particularly if the case goes to trial, since these groups are particularly skilled in supporting the victims of all sorts of crime.

RECOVERING FROM RAPE

Rape will affect you both physically and mentally. Physically, you may find that you have a discharge from your vagina and itching, too. You may also notice bruises, swollen areas and tenderness, which may not come up until hours later. It's important to go back to the same doctor to report them so that they are recorded. You are most likely to suffer psychologically after having been raped, but it affects women in different ways and at different times. Some girls go into a state of shock, others seem very calm and collected to begin with. Try not to feel guilty or ashamed; what happened wasn't your fault and guilt won't help your recovery. One of the most helpful emotions to feel is rage – it can be very cleansing and energizing – so don't be afraid to feel it.

It is common to feel that you do not want to be left alone, even for a few minutes. You may not be able to sleep, or you may want to simply go away and hide. All these feelings are perfectly normal. In time they will pass.

CHAPTER

LIVING

AT HOME

Once you have reached your teenage years, your relationship with your parents gradually evolves as they start to see you as an adult, which is something not all parents find easy to do. With luck, they'll encourage you to be independent and will respect your views, but there's bound to be friction from time to time, even in the happiest of families. In this chapter I offer advice on how you can resolve potentially difficult issues amicably, including staying out late, having a friend to stay, helping around the house, having a party and managing money.

PARENTS AND RELATIVES

For most of your adolescent years you have little option but to live with and be part of your family. Even when you get older and feel that you want to leave home, you will probably not be earning enough money to get by on your own – in fact, you may not be earning at all, so no matter how difficult relationships with your family may be, you've got to learn to rub along with them.

"Well they play fair with me so I play fair with them. I always tell them where I am at night and I don't stay out overnight without speaking to them first."

I say this not because I think you have great responsibilities to your family – some people have quite difficult parents and no-one would want you to stay with them longer than you absolutely had to – but learning to be part of a group is something that you're going to have to do at some time in your life anyway, and the earlier you learn to make a success of it the better. Even when you leave your family later for another group (say, if you share a flat with some friends), you're going to have to learn how to give and take, how to put your own wishes second, how to consider the views of others, and how to be helpful and co-operative. And the family is as good a place as any to learn these things.

GETTING ON WITH YOUR PARENTS

Most girls have quite close relationships with their mothers and may even get on better with them than with their fathers. As girls grow up, especially after the start of menstruation, it's quite common for an unspoken embarrassment to develop between fathers and their daughters that can last a long time. Don't worry if this happens to you, it's very common and you'll find that, in time, your relationship will change and improve.

"My mum and dad are all right. But I keep things very cool with them."

One of the best ways of getting along with your mother is to think of her as more of a friend than a parent; as a pal you'd go shopping with or have lunch with and who you'd confide in. Your mother will probably appreciate this and feel relieved that she can at last enjoy a more adult relationship with you. One way to get on to your parents' wavelength is to ask them what life was like when they were your age, what were the things that they could and couldn't do, and how they got on with their own parents. This approach may help your parents think back to their own teenage problems and, once they have related to you in this way, it will be extremely difficult for them to pull rank without trying to understand your point of view first. This doesn't mean that all the understanding has to go one way – it's your responsibility to try to understand them, too.

As they grow older, people get more resistant to change and this may be why parents often find it hard to change and are likely to be less flexible than you in their attitudes. Try to see their points of view, understand their backgrounds and what helped to produce their views. Even if you think that some of these views are plain stupid, don't say so in a loud or bitter voice. Try to be more persuasive and talk in a gentle, pleasant voice. If you control yourself, you'll find that your feelings cool down, you'll become less tense and angry and you will be far more likely to be able to sort things out amicably. Try this kind of approach with your parents several times and if it doesn't work, perhaps you should give the subject a rest and raise it again in a few months' time.

You may also find that a good way to get your parents to be a bit more understanding is to show them that other teenagers are just like you and want to do the same sorts of things. You could invite one or two friends to your house and then get either or both of your parents involved in a discussion so that your friends voice their opinions and views. Your parents will probably find your friends' views easier to accept because they are not emotionally involved and they can take a more objective view. If you find one parent harder to get on with than the other, you could try discussing your problems with the parent you're closest to and then say, "Well, do you think you could have a word with Mum/Dad?" That way, your more sympathetic parent can speak on your behalf with the other.

BROTHERS AND SISTERS

These are very important people in your life, because however much you fight now, try to bear in mind that, in future years, you will value their friendship and company, and they yours. When you're feeling at your worst, or they are behaving badly towards you, try to smile and say something pleasant. It's hard but it will pay off.

GETTING ON WITH OTHER RELATIVES

A lot of young people consider their uncles, aunts and grandparents to be a bit of a duty. They feel obliged to see them and only do so to keep the family peace. If this is the case with you, try to make an effort to show some respect, understanding and generosity towards them.

You'll be amazed, for example, how much a phone call, a short letter or a brief visit would mean to them. And it only costs you the minimum of time and effort to bring them so much pleasure. On the other hand, many teenagers find that they can build strong, close relationships with relatives and may even confide in them in a way that they can't with their own parents.

Grandparents, in particular, who have finished with the business of being parents themselves, now have time, leisure and patience to form relaxed friendships with their grandchildren. They can see everything in a far more objective way than they probably ever could with their own children.

Uncles and aunts who perhaps have no children of their own, can behave more like older brothers or sisters, and you may be able to build up valuable supportive relationships here, too.

YOUR GROWING INDEPENDENCE

Your parents will have been accepting your developing independence since you were a baby and most parents welcome the approach of maturity, encourage it and are proud of it. However, you may find that your parents are not so positive when you start to strike out for freedom, which can cause friction between you. If this is the case, you will need to use a little tact and subtlety towards them. Unless you plan ahead and introduce your parents gradually to the idea that you want to make decisions for yourself and manage your own life, you may end up having rows and destructive confrontations. You should try to avoid these at all costs. Introduce your desire for independence in a way that they can understand, for example, ask about what they wanted to do when they were the same age as you, and what their own parents allowed them to do. Ask them if they were happy with that situation and how they could have gone about getting more freedom. It should then be easier for your parents to see things from your point of view.

TAKING ON RESPONSIBILITIES

Your parents will be much more eager to accept your independence if you show them that you are responsible and trustworthy. You might, for instance, offer to take on some of the important jobs around the house. If your parents find that they can depend on you to cook the evening meal, to be a good babysitter or to carry out errands efficiently, then they will not only feel like giving you a little more independence but will also want to reward you by trusting your judgement.

One of the best ways to show your parents that you are a responsible person and can see a project through to the end is to take on some kind of part-time job. You could, for instance, take on a paper round when you are still in your early teens, and then later you could find a Saturday job, say, in a shop. This will clearly demonstrate that you are willing to work and that you can be responsible and possibly make a useful contribution to the household finances. Your parents may be grateful for the extra money, and they will certainly appreciate your gesture.

Babysitting
As well as being a great way to earn a little money, babysitting can demonstrate to your parents that you are responsible and trustworthy.

TALKING TO YOUR PARENTS

Every parent loves to be asked for advice, so if you have a problem, even if it's a minor one, consult your parents and ask them what you should do. In the beginning, you might start by talking about problems that are not too important to you so that you can listen to each other reasonably without getting angry. Your parents will get used to having this kind of dialogue and, when it comes to something that is important to you, they will be prepared to discuss it in a reasonable way.

One of the things that I have always found hard to resist with my own children is that, having been turned down once, they would then ask me again if they could attempt to do what they wanted to do. This had been going on since they were small children, when I used to stop them playing with dangerous things. As they grew older, they learned that once I had watched them accomplish difficult tasks and had seen that they were prepared to take precautions, there was no way that I could refuse them permission. Through patient negotiation with me they taught me to be reasonable. They were very proud of their achievement and I was also proud of them for having been persistent and sensible.

"The trouble is, adults never have any reason for making you do anything except for their own convenience."

Unless you cannot talk to your parents at all, or you find yourself always getting into arguments with them when you try to discuss things, I am sure that this "softly softly" approach is the one to take. If, however, you are one of those teenagers who simply cannot discuss matters with their parents without getting upset, I would be against your being independent and taking risks without consulting someone. You should try to find a trustworthy adult or older friend in your life to whom you can talk.

FEELING REBELLIOUS

Every teenager feels rebellious at some point; indeed, it's a normal part of growing up and trying to deal with all the emotional changes of adolescence. You may feel rebellious about the rules and regulations that society tries to impose on all of us, and closer to home, the rules and regulations that your parents want you to abide by while you're living with the family. Sometimes, you may feel that the give and take that is demanded of you and your brothers and sisters is unfair. Every teenager goes through these negative feelings, but not every teenager has rows and break-ups with their parents. You should try to fit in as much as possible and to get on with the rest of your family.

If you are feeling rebellious and angry, don't take it out on other people, simply say to those around you, "I want to be on my own" and leave the room, or "I'm just going out for a walk" and leave the house, or "I've got a bit of work to do" and go to your own room. This way, you'll attract more sympathy, understanding and respect from your parents. There's no need to verbalize your rebellious feelings, or to rant and rave to give vent to them. It's OK to lose your temper once in a while, after all most people get angry now and then, but not all the time.

HELPING AROUND THE HOUSE

I believe that all children should be doing chores around the house from a very early age. A family should be a team and team members need to help one another and give each other as much support as they can. As children get older, they can take responsibility for more and more difficult jobs and I think you should be on the look-out for opportunities that allow you to do this. Don't always wait for your parents to suggest ways in which you might help, or even for them to be forced to nag you before you take action. If you are observant and considerate, there are 101 tasks that you could take off their plates and their minds. Your parents would be very appreciative if you did a couple of chores on a regular basis, rather than only helping when you're in the mood, though occasional help is always welcome. So why don't you choose a few jobs that you enjoy doing (or you know they hate doing): it could be cleaning the car, doing a bit of gardening, helping with the baking or the ironing – anything, in fact, that gives your parents a bit of a break.

There are also several accomplishments that young people are often more familiar with than some parents, such as programming the video or using the Internet. Doing these kinds of tasks for your parents will not only make for a good relationship between you but it also allows your parents to show their appreciation by being fair and generous with you.

YOUR OWN SPACE

If space allows, all young people should have a place of their own in the home; a bolt hole where they can retire to and escape from the rest of the world. If you do have your own room, you should be proud of it; apart from anything else, it's a mark of respect for your own privacy by your parents. It can reflect your own personality with its colour scheme, furniture and the way that you decorate it. Don't forget that you are not living in a hotel – there isn't a maid who comes round to tidy your room each morning – and if it isn't tidied, your mother will almost certainly feel obliged to do it herself. You may well consider this an intrusion, but there is only one way round it: you owe it to the rest of the household to keep your room in a state of decent cleanliness and tidiness. It is not fair for you to say that as it's your room you can keep it as you like, dirt and all. There is no reason why your parents should tolerate your untidy room. It is fair and right for you to conform to their domestic standards while you are living at home. Perhaps you can come to some arrangement about keeping your room tidy and clean. You might decide that you do it at the weekend but during the week it can be as you leave it. Or you could do a swap with your mother. If there is a particular job that she doesn't like, why don't you offer to do it for her in exchange for her tidying your bedroom?

MAKING YOUR ROOM YOUR OWN

You can make a number of changes to your room that are quick and easy so that it becomes more like a bedsit and less like a bedroom: a nice place in which to work, sleep, relax, read or entertain your friends. You can divide the room into separate areas simply by using plants, bookcases or bead curtains. If any of the alterations you want to make involve painting the walls or otherwise making permanent changes to your room, make sure that you talk with your parents first. If you want to spend money on your room, see if your parents will help towards the cost of something expensive (say a sofabed), or whether they will let you "work off" the cost by taking on some extra jobs around the house. Remember that you may be able to buy second-hand rugs or bookshelves at junk shops or make some of the things cheaply yourself.

TIPS TO IMPROVE YOUR ROOM

If your bedroom still reflects an earlier age – get rid of the nursery wallpaper and toy clutter and bring it into line with your current needs.

Day bed/sofa *Scatter cushions and a throw-over cover can transform a single bed into a sofa.*

Windows *Inexpensive blinds look more up-to-date than traditional curtains.*

Work area *A piece of veneered chipboard or blockboard makes a useful, inexpensive worktop for study.*

Bookshelves *These can be easily constructed out of bricks and wooden boards.*

Seating *Get a sag or bean bag, which is comfortable to flop into, easy to move around, and fits into odd corners.*

Going out at night
When you are going out for the evening, as well as your house keys, it's a good idea to have a mobile phone with you for security.

YOUR NEEDS, RIGHTS AND PRIVILEGES

Some parents accept the argument that you should be allowed the same kind of freedom as your friends. Others do not. I personally feel that while you are living with your parents, you should do as they wish and stick to their rules. You will get nowhere if you deliberately go against what they have said. If you disagree, the only solution is to negotiate with your parents and come to some agreement whereby they give you increasing amounts of freedom while they learn to trust you.

If you think that your parents are being unreasonably strict, for instance, more strict than your friends' parents, then tell them that you think you're getting a rough deal, but also say that for the time being you accept this and ask if they would agree to a trial period with more freedom. If everything works out all right, then you could gradually introduce a few more privileges – always on the basis, of course, that you keep your promises.

STAYING OUT LATE

This is a contentious subject for all teenagers, both boys and girls, but it's worse for girls, largely because their parents tend to be more protective of them than of boys. You can do nothing to prevent this protective attitude, so be understanding and don't fly off the handle when this subject comes up.

Start discussions about it early and gradually. As you get older, you might ask your parents to allow you to stay out a little later if you tell them where you are, if you give them your phone number and if you promise to get home on time, and do so. Then you can justifiably ask them to let you stay out a bit later every few months. If you cheerfully volunteer information about your whereabouts, your parents will be greatly reassured.

GIVING PARTIES AT HOME

If you want to hold a party for your friends in your parents' house, there are some definite "do's" and "don'ts" to think about. Remember always that your parents are doing you a big favour by allowing you to hold a party in their house, so you should treat their property with respect and make sure that your friends do likewise. Don't be over-ambitious for your first party. Invite a modest number of people rather than a huge houseful, and don't expect your parents to let the party go on until 4.00 am. Also, don't do things that you know will upset your parents, such as drinking alcohol or playing the music too loudly and annoying the neighbours.

You might want to make a few rules for your friends, so that everyone knows exactly where they stand. For instance, you might ban smoking just in case people drop cigarette ends on to the carpet. However responsible you think your friends are, don't have the party in the best room in the house – your parents will rightly be angry if there's any damage, breakages or spoiling of furniture and carpets. Likewise, if your parents would rather you didn't use certain parts of the house, make sure that all your friends know those areas are out of bounds.

Whatever you do, don't have a party secretively when your parents are away from home, because they will easily guess what has been going on, never trust you again and you'll have ruined all your chances for giving parties in the future.

Preparation and precautions When you're clearing the room, remove anything of value before the party starts. If you think things may get broken, it's much better for your peace of mind to buy disposable paper cups and plates. If anything precious does get broken during the party, don't try to keep it a secret. Choose your moment soon after the party to tell your parents.

Don't allow gatecrashers into your party and, to keep strangers out, ask a couple of the boys to stay by the door. Don't let anyone sleep in the house after the party unless you have previously arranged this.

MANAGING MONEY

From quite an early age, it's important to get a feeling for the value of money and how you can use it. The best way of doing this is for your parents to start giving you weekly pocket money. If, by the time you get to your teens, your parents seem unsure of how much money to give you, find out from your friends what they're getting as pocket money. Ask your older friends by how much and when their pocket money increased over the years.

SHOULD YOUR PARENTS BE AT YOUR PARTY?

Sort out with your parents, as amicably as you can, whether they want to be at the party.

Most teenagers don't want their parents present, but most parents are scared, at least for the first time, about leaving their children to their own devices. You might be able to come to a compromise. For instance, your parents might go out for the evening, and you could arrange that they come back at a certain time.

Most parents want to help with the preparations; your mother may offer to do some of the food, and your father may want to help out with moving the furniture. But you and your friends may want to do everything yourselves, so work out these arrangements with your parents beforehand. It helps your parents to get into the swing of things if you have a few friends round to the house before the party to help do the food, decorate the room, clear the furniture, get the music set up and put shades on the lights.

If you're intending to have anything resembling a disco, introduce the person who's going to be doing it to your parents beforehand, especially if they are going to be using their precious equipment. Most disc jockeys tend to bring their own music but, if necessary, lock away all of your parents' special tapes and CDs.

FINANCIAL SUPPORT FROM PARENTS

While you're still living at home you can reasonably expect your parents to feed and clothe you and pay for your needs, provided that they aren't unreasonable.

However, you should always respect your parents' property. For example, if you and your friends go round to your house and use up the family's stock of bread and cheese in one sitting, then you should offer to replace the food out of your own money.

If you're going on to study for a higher qualification after school, you'll very likely need quite a lot of financial support from your parents. Don't think of this support as your inalienable right, it isn't, it's partly a gift from your parents. They want to do their best for you and they want to give you as much help as they can, so accept their help and thank them in a gracious way.

Personally, I feel that teenagers have a good case to argue that they should get some kind of financial support from their parents (though it may not be all that they need) until they finish studying and get a job. After that, I don't think that money should be free. If you need money, you can ask your parents for a loan that you will repay when you have a job. Or perhaps you can think of ways to pay them back as you go if money is short (see right).

Some parents believe in only giving their teenagers a little pocket money, but then pay for everything else when the need arises. Other parents give their teenagers more, sometimes in the form of an allowance, and then expect their children to pay for a lot more things themselves such as clothes and books.

One of the ways in which you could reach an agreement about pocket money with your parents is if you offer straightaway to put a little aside each week as a saving. Ask your parents to help you open a building society or bank account. It doesn't matter how small your saving is every week – whatever you can manage will show your parents that you're acting responsibly, and they will feel more amenable to giving you rises. But no matter how little pocket money you get, do keep aside a certain amount to spend on something that you really want.

I personally feel that if teenagers want to own large and expensive things, then they should contribute to them themselves. If you go to your parents and say, "If I can save half, would you pay for the rest?", your parent may say "Yes" straight away, or they may renegotiate the deal and say, "Well, you'll have to save up three-quarters of the amount, but I'll give you the rest". Or they may suggest giving you part of the amount as a birthday or Christmas present.

PAYING YOUR WAY

Whether it is to help pay for an expensive item you want or to pay back a loan from your parents while studying, you should think about ways to earn money. You could offer to do odd jobs around the house or garden or run errands for which you can be paid. If you are good at fixing things, for example, you could offer your services to the whole family to repair any appliance that breaks down for a certain sum of money.

I also believe that teenagers should try to do part-time jobs either in the evenings or at weekends to help pay their way. This does no harm at all, unless it makes you so tired that you can't find the time and energy for studying. Most American students pay their way through university with a bank loan, which they repay by taking jobs out of school hours. Another big advantage of having a job is that it gives you useful work experience early in life.

7

FAMILY CRISES

Most people grow up believing in "happy ever after"
endings, so discovering that your parents are separating
or divorcing can be very hard to bear. It may feel like the
end of the world, or that you'll never be happy again.
You may even think that it's partly your fault – many
children do – but this is simply not true. Never blame
yourself. In this chapter, I describe some strategies that
you might find helpful when coping with separation
and divorce and reassure you that your feelings and
reactions are normal. I also discuss ways of adjusting
to step-parents, and give useful advice on how to come
to terms with the death of a parent and what to do if
you are sexually abused.

YOUR EMOTIONS

You'll go through a whole host of conflicting emotions that nearly every teenager experiences when her family breaks up. It's OK to feel some or all of them.

- *You'll be feeling insecure.*

- *You may be scared that you'll have to live with the parent you like less.*

- *You'll be concerned about how a single parent will manage to look after you.*

- *You may go on worrying about whether both your parents will love you as they have done before. These are all very natural worries, but as time goes on, you'll find that a lot of them were unfounded and many of them are easier to deal with than you thought.*

"I don't think parents ought to stay together for the sake of the children. I've got a friend whose parents stayed together for the children's sake and it got worse and worse. They had separate food cupboards, separate times for eating their dinner, they wouldn't speak to each other and they had separate bedrooms."

SEPARATION OR DIVORCE

Although many people can claim to have a happy, carefree family life, many more do have problems at some point – some of them quite serious. The two most damaging blows that a family can experience are divorce and the death of a parent. While it's true that everyone involved in divorce suffers, in my view the children tend to be the ones who are most injured in the long run.

COPING WITH THE SITUATION

Adults have divorces, children don't, but it's just as hard for the children as it is for the parents, if not harder. No matter how young you may be when your parents' marriage is breaking up, you'll become increasingly aware of the strain and tension between them. One of the things that will hurt you most will be the quarrelling, the conflict and the uncertainty when parents are deciding whether to split up or not. In the past, expert advice has been very clear to parents: it said that it's best to stay together for the sake of the children, and this often meant continuing quarrels, or, even worse, parents staying together who were cold, loveless and indifferent towards each other. You may well feel that there's no point in parents staying together under one roof simply for the sake of appearances, and nearly all children feel that on balance it would have been better if parents had split up earlier and been more honest with them.

It's very hard for teenagers to live in a house where you never see your parents touch or kiss one another, or where you have to explain their separate bedrooms. Sometimes the strain is intolerable, especially as you often pick up small changes in atmosphere which your parents think you don't notice.

If your parents' marriage is breaking up, you'll probably be very aware of the atmosphere of recrimination and silence. Perhaps when you're in bed late at night listening to parental fights or arguments you'll feel frightened and helpless. Don't fall into the trap of thinking that the arguments are about you and that you are in some way to blame. You're not a burden to your parents, and in no way is the tense atmosphere in the home your fault. If your parents won't tell you what's going on, try to confide in an older friend or an older relative and ask him or her to speak to your parents.

If you're living in a tense, unhappy atmosphere at home, and even if your parents are arguing most of the time and are violent, it may not enter your head at first that a divorce is the remedy. You'll probably feel that you just want them to stop quarrelling and have a more peaceful and predictable way of life, but this may not be possible and eventually even you will come to the conclusion that separation or divorce is the only way.

Feelings about separation When you do hear the news that your parents are going to separate, you may find yourself feeling conflicting emotions. It's normal to feel confused because on the one hand you'll want your parents to stay together, and yet you may also feel relieved, even pleased, that a bad situation is going to end, even though you feel threatened because your familiar world seems to be breaking up.

Nearly all adolescents feel angry with a parent who breaks up the home or who deserts them. You may feel particular resentment towards the parent who, in your judgement, was responsible for the break-up of the marriage. You may even feel so angry that you reject the parent who you believe is guilty and refuse to see him or her, even if he or she comes to the house to see you.

You may feel that you want to hide the fact that your parents are separated. You may feel that coming from a broken home is shameful, and that in some way it makes you different. If you live within a community in which divorce is frowned on, then you may even feel that people will think badly of you. If you feel like this, turn to an older relative who knows you well, one of your grandparents, for instance, who will reassure you on this matter and tell you that your happiness and the ultimate happiness of your parents is what matters and not other people's opinions.

Alternatively, it would also be quite normal for you to feel greatly relieved because at least now there'll be no more quarrelling or violence at home, and you'll know that a bad situation has probably ended.

COMMON REACTIONS

Here are some of the typical reactions that teenagers feel when their parents decide on divorce. Those feelings that are most commonly reported are listed first:

- *Unhappiness and depression*
- *Tearfulness*
- *Bewilderment*
- *Relief*
- *Feeling different to others*
- *Wanting to take sides and blame one parent*
- *Insecurity*
- *Indifference*
- *Guilt*

"I knew something was wrong. I heard arguments when I was in bed and I cried. I didn't know too much because I was too young to realize what it was all about. My mother was depressed. She had to wear dark glasses because she was always crying."

HOW YOUR PARENTS SHOULD BEHAVE

There are many things that parents should and shouldn't do in a divorce but sadly, they are not perfect, and sometimes they may overlook your needs. It may help to go through the following wish list with them:

● *Both parents should show that they love you and still want to be involved in your life.*

● *Both parents should arrange to see you regularly and on a basis that you understand.*

● *Both parents should spend time with you, take you away for weekends and holidays, and see you during the week.*

● *The parent you live with should be supportive and not obstruct your relationship with the other parent.*

● *Parents should realize that it's easier for you to continue a relationship with both of them if they are friendly to each other.*

WHAT YOUR PARENTS SHOULDN'T DO

Children feel love and loyalty for both parents, so it's distressing if they're "used" by one parent to get at the other.

● *One parent should never run the other parent down or try to turn their children against the other parent.*

● *Parents should not use emotional blackmail or try to use you to get information.*

You may eventually feel that your parents will be happier apart than they were together. Perhaps you'll no longer have to protect one of your parents and you won't have to cope with tension and uncertainty. The atmosphere in the home will be more peaceful and you'll be able to concentrate on your homework, get on with school life and start socializing with your friends again.

Then again, you may feel nothing very dramatic at all. You may be looking for feelings that you don't have. You may not feel relieved, and you may not feel any dismay. You may feel quite indifferent and that's normal, too. After all, when your parents separate, there may not be any great changes. You may still live in the same house and still see both parents.

At the time of the break-up, you'll probably find that you want far more detailed explanations than your parents are prepared to give you. You'll probably also want more and different information as you grow up. Research shows that few parents realize the needs of their teenage children, so it's going to have to be you who initiates discussions. Try to make talks and explanations part of a continuing process of recovery. If necessary, ask your parents to respond to your changing need for information, otherwise you may end up feeling like this girl: "I know she said he'd left for another woman, but I can't remember my Mum actually sitting down and talking to us about it. I'm sure she did, but I can't remember now. I would have liked to talk more about it, especially when things calmed down a bit. I wanted to know what really happened because now I'm older I can understand more."

What you may find strange is that your separated parents may not understand that you'll want to continue relationships with both of them. You must try to impress on your parents that you only have one Mum and Dad and that you love both of them.

Deciding who to live with Unless you have a marked preference for one of your parents and really don't get on with the other, it will be quite difficult to decide which parent to live with. For instance, although you prefer your father, you may feel you have a responsibility to your mother, to make sure that she's all right and to help out with any difficulties she may have. You may also feel that if you choose to live with one parent, you'll upset the other. Many teenagers are worried about this, but when you're making this very difficult decision you have to try to be more selfish than you might reasonably feel you can be. You've got to put your own happiness higher up on your priority list. You have to live your own life. Don't forget that your parents are grown up and are supposed to be able to take care of themselves. Furthermore, it's not your fault if they can't. So the parent that you feel it's right for you to live with is the one that you are happiest with.

Working this out may not be straightforward. In a divorce, one parent is nearly always given care of the children, which means that even if your parents have joint custody and all decisions about welfare, schooling and so on are made jointly, one parent becomes the primary carer. So generally speaking, this means that one of your parents will have to look after you most of the time. You'll probably have to live in one house for most of the week, go to the same school every day and sleep at one house most of the time. The possibility of your being able to "share" your life equally between your two parents is very unlikely, although you may be able to spend weekends and holidays with the other parent.

I believe that once you are over the age of 12, you should be able to decide which parent you live with. Your opinion should be sought, but if it is not, you should make sure that both your parents are clear about your preference. If you find that you are being ignored, seek the help of an older relative or an older friend or even a teacher and ask her or him to intervene so that your views are at least considered.

If you're aged 16 or over, it's much easier because you have a right to decide which parent you want to live with. You also have the right to take legal advice and a solicitor will be able to help you if this is a difficult problem. In fact, you should not have to resort to this, but teenagers have done so where necessary. If you possibly can, you should try to make your views clearly known to both parents and then, through discussion, try to arrange your life so that you can live happily with whom you want and where you want.

DON'T BLAME YOURSELF

You may think that you yourself are the cause of the break-up. You may also feel rejected and blame yourself for this. It's never your fault, and try to believe that. It's an awful feeling, but as time passes, you'll feel less responsible and less guilty.

You may harbour the thought that if you'd behaved differently your parents would still be together, but this simply is not true.

You'll find it very difficult not to blame both your parents for betraying the whole family and you may find that you blame most the parent who leaves home. But remember that the situation is not simple; it's very complicated and it's nearly always both parents who are responsible for the break-up of their marriage.

"If the father's going to go away he should come and see the children regularly so that they know him and so that they can speak to him and tell him what's going on."

SEPARATION FROM BROTHERS AND SISTERS

If you are separated from your brothers and sisters because of divorce or death, you may feel that your life has become more unbearable.

We all rely on our brothers and sisters more than we think. Very often they may just seem to be an irritation and a thorn in the flesh, but we can usually go to them for company, for moral support, for new ideas and to hear about their experiences.

There are sometimes very deep relationships between brothers and sisters, which, if broken, causes great unhappiness. If things go badly for your family, whatever you do, don't lose touch with your brothers and sisters. Telephone them when you can or write letters to them as often as possible.

You can gain tremendous comfort from just hearing a familiar voice or from getting a letter in return. Remember that your brothers and sisters will be going through the same agonies as you are, and it will help you all if you get together and compare notes about your feelings. Only your brothers and sisters have the same experience of your parents and family as you, and this common bond will give you great strength.

Facing up to changes All of us need security. Disruption of the familiar routine in our daily lives is scary, but it's much better if you are able to face up to the fact that there are going to be changes in your life and that some of these changes are unavoidable. However, try not to be too negative about it all. It will help you a great deal if you and your parents can face the changes together and make joint plans with an optimistic outlook.

Moving house may be one of the most disruptive and unpleasant events you will have to face, but you can be prepared for it. Talk to your parents about how this will affect you in practical terms. For example, it's possible you may have to change schools; you may not be able to see your old friends any more; it may not be so easy to see your other parent's relatives, and you may also find that your new home is different so that you can't have a bedroom of your own and you lack the privacy you're used to. Your new house may not be as nice as the old one. There may also be more than one move. If you realize that your housing conditions are deteriorating as a result of separation or divorce, you may feel angry, sad or deprived. Don't forget that your parents may be feeling exactly the same.

Regaining your confidence When your parents split up you may feel weak and vulnerable and that you've lost all your confidence, particularly about meeting friends and building up relationships. If so, it's easy to lock yourself into a little world of your own to protect yourself against being hurt more, and you may find yourself getting defensive, wary of new relationships and reluctant to trust people. Being slow to make friends is a common problem. Despite this, quite a few teenagers feel that there's a positive side to the split-up and that they have made personal gains. For instance, if your mother has to go out to work now and you have to look after younger brothers and sisters or help more with running the home, your responsibilities will have increased. This may help you feel mature and as a result more self-reliant and confident.

You'll be really mature and grown up if you can realize too that although your parents are divorced, they were once happy together, and the divorce has not cancelled out all the positive aspects of their marriage. This will help you to come to terms with the break-up of the family, giving you new confidence to make new relationships.

DEATH OF A PARENT

The death of one of your parents is the worst thing that can happen to you. Through all the pain, the grief and the confusion, you can carry the certain knowledge that if you can survive this, you can survive anything.

THE EARLY DAYS

Most children find it hard to believe that one of their parents has really died. After it happens, you may occasionally, perhaps when reading a book, forget and think that your parent is still somewhere around the house. You may imagine things that you're going to do with him or her, then suddenly you'll stop and remember that your parent isn't there any more.

It is very difficult to cope with death and if your parent dies suddenly or violently it's likely to affect you even more than if your Mum or Dad had a long illness that gave you time to prepare together. For the first day and night afterwards, it's better not to be alone. Try to stay with your other parent, your brothers and sisters or close relations. It's normal to feel scared and insecure at this time, so being with people you love will help you.

You may find that in grief the family draws very close together, literally huddles together. Physical closeness is very comforting, so hug everyone as much as you can. I remember one story of a father and two sons who'd lost their precious Mum all sleeping together in the same bed for the first week after she died.

Attending the funeral To save your feelings, your parent and relatives may not want you to go to the funeral, but if you want to go, it's very important for you to be there, so insist on it. It will help you enormously if you can be involved in the funeral arrangements and funeral service, for example, choosing flowers, music and readings. If possible, ask to see your parent's body beforehand as well – the funeral director will arrange this for you.

Though it's very hard, you'll get over your parent's death more quickly if you see the burial or cremation and have a chance to say your personal goodbye. Later, you'll get comfort from visiting the grave or garden of remembrance. You may find it easier to come to terms with their absence if you can see the grave.

TALKING ABOUT WHAT HAPPENED

Even if it's painful at first, you'll eventually want to talk about how your Mum or Dad died. Adults are often afraid to talk to children in case it's upsetting for them, but it can be easier if you make the first move. It'll be a great comfort to know what really happened, and to find out the circumstances of your parent's death.

You may wonder if your Mum or Dad is keeping something from you, so ask questions for your own peace of mind. Not knowing what happened can be terrible, and in a way it's as though you're in suspense all the time. Getting the facts may clear your head and help you deal with your raging emotions. It's not just kinder, it's better to know the full story. Explain this to your parent.

HOW YOU WILL FEEL

It's normal to have lots of different feelings after the death of someone very close to you. At first you may feel shock, then denial (you can't accept that it's happened), then anger, and finally sadness and depression. You may feel so miserable that you just want to withdraw from the world, not wanting to speak, see anyone or do anything. You may just want to sit in a chair in your own room and think. Many hours can pass quite quickly while you're in this mood, and comfort from brothers and sisters and the rest of the family doesn't seem to mean anything. You may not want to go to school or even to go out; you'll just want to be alone with your thoughts.

For a few weeks this is perfectly normal and you should ask people to let you go through this state of shock and grieving on your own if you want to. However, at the end of two weeks or so you might want to start getting back to your normal routine. Try to mix in with the family again and go out occasionally, perhaps to see a film. It's a good idea also to organize your school books and sports gear so that you can make an attempt to start ordinary living again.

However, remember that if you continue to feel low and depressed for some time, it's not abnormal. It's understandable, too, if you feel afraid of being alone, even of going to the bathroom or your bedroom on your own. You may have difficulty going to sleep and want someone close to you to cuddle. It's natural to want to be close to your Mum or Dad, but this may not always be feasible. So explain that you're frightened, don't be shy to say that you've suddenly got scared of the dark again because even adults do that, and ask if you could have a friend or a relative to stay who could sleep near you, in the same room or the same bed.

HOW YOUR FRIENDS MAY REACT

Don't be surprised if your friends find it difficult to deal with your parent's death, if they don't quite know how to say sorry and have difficulty starting sentences because they feel embarrassed about mentioning the subject of death. They may be scared that if they do bring up the subject, you'll be upset and start crying, and then they won't know what to do. You may find that friends turn away or drop their eyes when they meet you. It may even look as though they're crossing the street so that they don't have to face you.

Your close friends should know better, but you can also do a lot to put them at ease. You can approach them and start talking. You'll feel a lot more comfortable if you clear the air by saying something like, "You know that my mother died, but it's all right, we don't have to talk about it". You may get annoyed with friends who seem to pity you. No-one likes to be pitied and no-one likes to feel that their friends have to be protective. Don't worry that they'll think you're helpless, they'll soon realize you're not. They'll also appreciate that you're not very different from the person you were before. If you find that someone tries to be overprotective or continually tries to comfort you, be honest and ask them to stop, and they will.

WHAT YOU CAN DO

Crying can help. Sometimes crying together with your Mum or Dad can help both of you. You'll probably come across your parent doing something and crying at the same time. Don't be embarrassed, just go across and hold your Mum or Dad; this can bring you closer together than you were before, you'll comfort each other and be stronger afterwards. Having a family chat every now and then can help you

When your world ends
Nothing can prepare you for the death of a parent. But don't suffer alone – talk about it – with family, friends or, if necessary, with bereavement counsellors who can help you recover.

get your feelings out in the open. You can talk about what's happened, how you feel and what you're going to do for the future. There's a lot of truth in the old saying, "a trouble shared is a trouble halved", so you'll just feel a lot better for having talked about your feelings. You may find that your brothers and sisters are feeling exactly the same as you and you won't feel so alone.

Keeping a diary is a great comfort, too. Your diary can be like a friend who'll listen to you without arguing. You can put a lot of your secret thoughts down on paper when it's too difficult to talk about them. It's a huge relief to get those thoughts out of your mind. Once they're in the diary, it's as though you've dealt with them: they're over and you don't have to experience the pain any more.

DEALING WITH YOUR WORRIES

When one of your parents has died, you may find that all sorts of things start to worry you which didn't before. It's normal to worry about your Mum or Dad's welfare, and you may even worry whether they're going to die too. If your parent died of an illness, it's normal to worry whether the illness runs in the family or not. Talk to your doctor about this, and if you are really anxious, ask to see a bereavement counsellor.

You may worry about much smaller things too. Will you suddenly not have enough money, will you have to leave your house, will you see your friends again, who will pick you up from school, who will get your lunch, who will look after you at the weekend, who will make sure you have a clean sports kit, who will give you your pocket money, who will help you do your hair? Don't let small problems overcrowd your mind, concentrate on one at a time. Deal with the one that you think is the most serious and you'll find that the smaller ones take care of themselves without your even noticing. You'll also realize that a lot of people can help you with your worries and difficulties.

How activity helps One way in which you can relieve your anxiety is to start making lists of things that you can do to help yourself. Be practical, make plans of the various steps that you have to take in order to solve what seems to be a particularly difficult problem. You'll find that when you've written things down on paper there are usually several possible solutions. There may be two or three solutions that you think will work and, with a little bit of hard work and effort on your part, you can actually carry out. Making plans and taking action are the two best ways of overcoming your anxiety, so when you're in a spot, get a piece of paper and a pencil and start writing down possible solutions and action plans. In my view, it never fails to help.

After one of your parents has died, you may find that you have more responsibility and more work to do at home. You may have to take care of your younger brothers and sisters. You may have to look after your mother or father, or feel that you should. You may feel that you have to fill a gap that your dead parent has left, helping with chores, jobs around the house, and doing lots of errands. In a way, this will help you get over your grief. Helping someone is healing too.

LIFE AFTER DIVORCE OR DEATH

If your mother wants to or has to get a job, it could be a real help because it would bring her into contact with new friends and colleagues. Even if you want her to be at home for you, she'd feel so much better if you told her that it wouldn't be fair for her to stay at home alone just to look after you.

"A few days ago, I was talking to my mother and she asked me how I'd feel if another man liked her and she liked him and they got married. I said as long as they're happy it was OK, but that there would never be another father like my father."

One of the things that you're bound to find difficult to face up to is if your parent meets a new partner and maybe wants to re-marry. It's natural to feel that this is not fair to the memory of your other parent because you know in your heart that no-one can replace them for you. But try to put yourself in the position of your Mum or Dad, who's lonely and needs a special friend for help and support. You know how loneliness feels, and if you think about it, you'll soon understand that it wouldn't be fair for your parent to be alone for the rest of her or his life.

Living with a lone parent Being part of a one-parent family is hard on everybody. More and more fathers are taking on the care and parenting of their children, which may mean that, with a young family, they even have to give up their jobs and live on state benefits. But as a general rule, it's harder on a single-parent family if the lone parent is a woman. A single woman with young children often finds it hard to find employment that has flexible enough hours to fit in with school, or that offers a salary large enough to enable her to pay for child care. However, if you are into your teens when your parent loses a partner, your new-found independence may be a great help here.

Parental worries You'll soon realize that your parent's main worry is about daily necessities. You'll probably notice that your Mum or Dad goes without things to make sure that you're provided for. Be aware that your Mum or Dad worries if they have to deprive you of clothes and outings and all the kinds of things that better-off children get. Be sympathetic and be as helpful as you can and try not to complain. Remember that your parent finds it very hard to refuse your requests for money or treats, and probably feels full of guilt whenever he or she has to refuse you. Don't forget that if your parent has to deprive you, they may feel insecure and concerned that they'll damage their relationship with you or even lose your love.

Standing on your own feet With only one parent in the family, a lot of responsibility – not just for yourself, but for others if you've got younger brothers and sisters – may now fall on your shoulders. Everyone is going to have to buckle down and work for the good of the family. There has to be a lot of team spirit and very little selfishness and you're going to have to stand on your feet earlier than you otherwise would have done.

You're going to have to learn to make decisions and to do chores and jobs to help your parent in making sure that the family runs smoothly.

If you are old enough, you may feel that you should try to get a part-time job so that there's more money to go round. You may also have to take up new (unpaid) duties for the family such as cooking or child-minding. You may have to learn to mend items instead of buying new ones and to deal with money in a responsible way. Try to feel proud of doing these things rather than dismayed. It may seem tough now, but in the long term, it could be a big bonus to have acquired these skills.

Family budget
When money's tight, every little helps and there are many ways you can help family finances, from not wasting food or electricity, to getting a part-time job.

STEP-PARENTS

Adjusting to a step-parent is one of the most difficult things a child has to do. It's natural and understandable to see new people as intruders who disturb your family, and steal your parent's love and attention. You may feel not only emotionally threatened, even pushed aside in your own home, but also that your space has been invaded by a stranger.

It's very hard for you to cope with what seems to be the loss of your parent's affection, particularly if you're fearful that the new partner will try to play the role of the parent who has left you. You may feel resentment and anger, and resist their new authority.

You'll probably discover, however, that many step-parents don't set themselves up as rival mother- or father-figures, and that they'll make you feel valued and important. On many occasions, you'll find that you get special attention. You may even realize that your home with your step-parent is more stable and better organized than it was when your parent managed alone. Your step-parent may help you to feel that you're cared for, that your opinions are sought and listened to and that you're treated more like an adult.

Sometimes it's a relief when your parent gets a new partner, whether or not they marry again, because it's nice to know that your parent's life is easier. You'll probably also feel a sense of relief that you don't have to bear the responsibility for his or her loneliness and unhappiness.

Step-brothers and step-sisters When your parent begins a new relationship, you may also acquire step-sisters and step-brothers. Not everyone finds this straightforward and you may experience rivalries and conflicts. Don't think that you're unusual if there are quarrels and skirmishes with your step-brothers and step-sisters; time and contact will make things a lot easier. It's likely that at first you may feel that they are not really members of the family and that they seem more like distant cousins, but once you don't feel like strangers to each other, it'll be easier to become friends.

MAKING THINGS EASIER

This situation is always complicated and at first you'll probably hate sharing your home with new people. Despite all the problems, however, step relationships can work. Here are several ideas that may help you:

● *Be sympathetic. Your step-brothers and step-sisters are probably feeling as confused and insecure as you.*

● *Try to look towards the future; things do get better.*

● *Make a list of all the things that upset you, then ask if you can have a chat with everyone about the situation.*

● *Be positive about the good things, and when someone does something nice or kind, tell them so.*

You and your new family
You may not think so at first, but a step-family will provide you with the support and love you need.

SEXUAL ABUSE AND INCEST

Incest is the term for sexual relations between close relatives; sexual abuse can also occur with someone who is not related to you but who is part of your everyday life, especially someone who is close to you and who has some authority over you. The most common relationship of this type is between step-father and daughter.

Sexual abuse may start when you're very young, as young as five or six. At this age, you generally accept what adults say and do as right, and you go along with what an adult asks you to do. You may even think that it's normal and natural and that other people do the same. As you get older, you will realize that the relationship is wrong. You may feel that it's very unpleasant and want to escape from it. However, as you're involved with an adult who is in control of things, it may be difficult to find a way out. You may also feel too afraid to tell anyone because you think that no-one will believe what you say, or that they will blame you for what has happened.

Many girls who are sexually abused say that they feel somehow that they're to blame for this abnormal relationship. They believe there is something about themselves that encouraged it and that made the adult do certain things. If you are abused, you may also feel terribly guilty because you feel responsible for this awful situation in the family and are frightened of the consequences. You may also feel guilty because the relationship is dishonest and because you are keeping something bad from your mother.

No abused child or teenager is ever responsible for the abusive actions of an adult, so try to come to terms with the fact that it really isn't your fault. It's very important that you seek help, whether it has happened to you in the past or whether it is happening now. The first thing you should do is tell someone and this will stop the abuse (see column, left).

If you can talk to someone and eventually get help from a counsellor who is specialized in this area, you may find that you can resolve your feelings of anger, guilt, shame and depression about what has happened and you can look towards the future with confidence.

SCHOOL AND CAREER

When you're wading through piles of homework while your friends are out enjoying themselves and have plenty of money, dropping out of school can seem like a tempting idea. But before you do, remember that a good education is priceless. At school you can discover new subjects, talents and interests, and gain qualifications that can be the key to all the most interesting jobs. In this chapter, I discuss the advantages of continuing your education, how to study effectively and how to deal with exams. I also explore your options when you leave school, including going to university and choosing a career.

A GOOD EDUCATION

There's simply no question that a good education is the best tool a girl can have to help her manage her life, achieve happiness and enjoy some degree of freedom. Life beyond school is not perhaps as straightforward as it used to be – even some university graduates with good degrees have difficulty in finding jobs. In order to get on and overcome the obstacles that will inevitably lie in your path, you have to have a strong belief that educating yourself is a priority in your life.

WHAT AN EDUCATION CAN OFFER

It wasn't until I was through my adolescent years that I realized that continuing my education offered me the kind of freedom that nothing else in my life possibly could. With qualifications, it was possible to apply for jobs that paid enough so that I didn't have to worry about paying for basic needs like a roof over my head, food and clothing. My education made me strong and independent, not just financially, but emotionally and intellectually. With it, I had the ability to follow my preferences and exercise my options.

Having an education also means that you will always have interests to fall back on during low or lonely points in your life because it will give you a vast fund of inner resources. It should also mean that you will be able to analyse problems, sort out solutions and expedite actions at work, in the community and in your social life.

Educating boys and girls Most schools today are co-educational, and have teachers of both sexes. It used to be thought that girls did better overall in single-sex schools, but because of changing attitudes within education, schools are now much more aware of the dangers of gender stereotyping. This has had an enormously beneficial effect on girls' educational achievements – in recent years, it's become clear that up to the age of 16, girls do better than boys in all subjects, whether they are at single-sex schools or not.

However, with boys around in school it means that you will be continually aware of the differences between you and them. Boys can be very distracting during lessons and, in class, if teachers aren't careful, boys still tend to dominate class discussions, and may demand more of the teacher's time, because on the whole girls are better at getting on with their work unsupervised.

Getting on at school Everyone has a few problems at school. There may be teachers you don't get on with and subjects that you don't like. You may find that certain lessons are beyond you. However, don't let these problems dominate; it's worth bearing in mind that, overall, girls achieve better results and do better in examinations than boys throughout most of their school life.

For many girls, the desire to conform with their girl-friends may distract them from study even more than thinking about boys, and they tend to see achievement in terms of their appearance, social life and popularity instead of their academic abilities.

As you progress through school and possibly on to further education, it's sometimes tempting just to give up and have time to enjoy yourself. Try not to be influenced by friends who've given up studying, who've left school early to get a job or feel that marriage and a family at 18 is what's right for them. Remember that they, not you, are the ones who may be narrowing their options for the rest of their lives.

SCHOOL WORK AWAY FROM SCHOOL

Most people have to do a great deal of hard work and study for many hours to prepare for exams. You often have several subjects to study, and this work can seem a real chore. If you don't love information for its own sake, and very few people do, then the most practical way of looking at this work is that it has to be done to give you the freedom to do what you want later on. It's a grind that you've just got to go through.

It's good for you to learn determination and staying power early in your educational career because you're going to need a great deal of these qualities later on if you're going to hold down a job successfully.

Fitting it in There's no doubt that while you're having to study in the evenings, you'll sometimes feel jealous and resentful about those of your friends who are not studying, who may have left school and have jobs and money and who go out every night apparently without a

School projects
As part of your course work, you may have to research and write up a project. This teaches you useful skills for the future.

care in the world. You're not unique; everyone who studies has experienced this, and many girls before you have ignored it, continued to study and become successful.

The right amount of homework Most young people are expected to do about two hours' home study an evening during the week, plus three to four hours at weekends, and probably some extra project work during holiday periods. Your school should guide you as to the amount of homework you are supposed to do. If very little homework is being given to you, or you're finding that you can do what you're given on the bus home, it's not going to do you much good in the long run. However, if you suddenly realize that you're doing three or four hours a night and more at weekends, you may be overloading yourself or working too slowly. Talk to your parents and teachers about maintaining a balance or possibly learning how to work faster.

WHY HOMEWORK HELPS

When you do homework, you are understanding and consolidating what you have been taught during the day. Although you may think homework is a chore, it can be the road to great achievements because, as well as providing the information to do well in exams, it teaches you many personal skills.
- Homework teaches you how to study independently without guidance and how to use your own judgement.
- It teaches you discipline, not only the discipline of routine, but discipline in the way you have to tackle your work, plan it out, present it and write it out.
- When you have a difficult or long assignment to complete against a deadline, it teaches you persistence and determination – qualities that every girl needs in ample supply if she is to follow a demanding career in a competitive world.
- Learning to manage your school work alongside outside interests and the normal social life that all girls need and enjoy actually prepares you for the world of work (and motherhood) later, by instilling such skills as time management and the ability to handle pressure.
- All of these achievements will bring you a sense of self-respect and confidence, not to mention the pride that your parents and teachers will feel in your successes.

Studying sensibly
When exams are imminent, you may have to do many hours of homework. Make yourself a study timetable, with plenty of regular breaks, and stick to it.

COPING WITH TESTS AND EXAMINATIONS

It wasn't until I was doing my medical finals at the age of 23 that I really came to terms with answering examination papers, so here are a few tips that you might like to consider:

• If you possibly can, plan your answer roughly and write it out briefly in pencil on a piece of spare paper. Make a list of all the points you're going to make. Even put down those points that may seem irrelevant. While you're writing, your notes will jog your memory to remember facts that are relevant. If you can bear to do this first of all, you'll find that you'll relax. Your nerves will become steadier and your brain will start ticking over much more clearly and quickly. You will free your brain from nervousness and all your energy can then be directed towards answering the question.

• It may take you 20 to 25 minutes to do this planning and you may see people around you scribbling away already, getting their answers down. Don't be deterred – it really does pay off. If you are allowed to, leave all your planning papers clipped to your exam papers and your examiners will see that you have gone to the trouble to plan your answers out beforehand and that you have an orderly mind. At the end of 25 minutes, you can relax a little because in fact you've got the answer to the question, all that remains now is to write it out in full. While you're writing, thoughts will come into your memory that will enhance the outline that you've scribbled down in pencil.

• Cut down the examiner's work. He or she will be on your side if your paper is easy to read and mark. Clear writing is essential. Leave spaces between thoughts, perhaps a couple of lines. The examiner will learn very quickly that you're making a new point each time and will take in each point more easily.

• If you can, answer the whole question in summary in the first sentence or first paragraph. In this way you will be letting the examiner know that you understand what the question is getting at and you have a good idea of the required answer.

• Depending on the subject, you'll get several marks for a clear diagram because it implies that you have digested information well enough to put it into graphic form.

MAKING SPACE FOR HOME STUDY

Your studies are important and if domestic arrangements allow, you should make sure that the rest of the family understands that study is one of your main priorities.

You will need:

• *A quiet space. If you're going to study for long hours alone, it's only fair that you have a room or at least a space in which you can study, that is quiet, comfortable and well heated.*

This room will probably be your bedroom but wherever it is it should be a calm place that is recognized by everyone as being yours and where disturbances are minimal.

• *Adequate furniture. You need a minimum of furniture such as a desk, a few drawers or shelves for your files and equipment and some shelves for your schoolbooks and reference texts.*

• *A good reading light and a comfortable chair that gives you good support.*

- If a question has several parts, check through your plan to make sure you'll be covering each part. If it's appropriate, insert sub-headings at the beginning of each separate section.
- Make sure that your final answers have a beginning, a middle and an end. If you are writing an essay, you should plan an introduction in which you set out the ideas that you are going to cover, a development in which you discuss the ideas in detail, and a conclusion to round everything off and tie up ends.
- Try to allow ten minutes or so to read through your answers at the end. It's too easy when writing at speed to misspell or even leave words out simply because your brain is working faster than your hand, and you can pick up slips like this that may make the difference between a lower or higher grade in your final result.
- If you find that you have to answer a question about which you know very little, don't panic, start jotting down everything you've ever heard about that subject, whether it was on television, in a magazine, in an encyclopedia, chatting to friends or from talking to your parents. While you're writing, more things may occur to you and you may remember some of the things you were taught in class or did in the laboratory.

SURVIVING YOUR STUDIES

There's no point in saying that it's easy for a young person to survive hard days at school and long hours working at night, especially when the rewards aren't immediately forthcoming or easy to see. It isn't. It takes a lot of staying power, a lot of grit, guts and determination. It also takes resilience. There will be times when you'll feel depressed and think that it's just not worth the effort. Well, no-one can give you the will to carry on and the will to succeed. You're going to have to find that somewhere inside of yourself.

If you feel that your willpower is cracking, have a chat to the teachers you most respect and ask them for tips. Most schools nowadays know that examinations can be especially stressful and will provide revision classes and advice on how to cope.

Ask your teachers, your parents or other adults you know who have been successful academically about the frustration and resentment that they've felt themselves.

You won't feel so bad when you hear that somebody who's achieved their career goals went through the same thing as you are experiencing.

Looking after yourself At the same time, don't work to the point of getting ill or having a nervous breakdown. Nothing is worth that; your health is the most important possession you have, so look after yourself. If you really feel that work is taking too much out of you, that you're not sleeping properly, that you can't eat or you're losing weight, or you're getting very strung up, then ease off for a while. Look at your priorities and find time to relax in front of the television or read a book that's got nothing to do with what you're studying.

FINDING TIME TO RELAX

When your work is over, take time off and relax. To stop feeling guilty that you're not working, give yourself deadlines, for example, so many pages to learn, so many words to write, so many sides to cover or so many words of vocabulary to memorize, and once you've reached your goal, you can feel that you've earned the time to have some fun.

Play hard Take part in as many activities as you can. Join in with groups of friends so that your mind is distracted. Do fun things and wear fun clothes. Another way to relax yourself completely and immediately is to take some form of exercise; even walking for half an hour will calm your nerves, relieve a headache and give you lots of energy. If you take exercise regularly, you'll find that you're able to go on for much longer in the evening without getting tired. You'll also be able to enjoy parties, stay on until the end of the disco, do with a few hours' sleep and yet wake fresh in the morning.

Enjoy life
Take a break from studying to relax with your friends. Sharing a joke and having a chat will recharge your batteries.

WHAT IF YOU DON'T SUCCEED?

Many girls fear failure. In fact, fear of failure may be one spur that keeps girls working diligently and sticking at their studies when boys give up. Typically, a girl may find that she prefers to return and repeat a task that she's already done successfully, and this may mean she's holding herself back. Boys nearly always prefer to move on to a new task, and this is an important way of learning and gaining self-confidence. Furthermore, don't believe that success depends more on chance and the whims of others than on yourself. To be successful you have to believe in yourself, your ability, and be able to cope with success.

GETTING HELP

If you're having difficulty in a subject or subjects, don't be afraid to admit to your teacher that you need help. A good school will have been monitoring your progress and hopefully have picked up problems early, but if you suddenly find you're getting behind or perhaps have missed out because of illness, you must ask for help. If the teaching staff have high expectations of you, and you are actually having difficulty, they need to know.

Vocational training Academic ability is not the only path to a good career and it would be wrong if you saw it as such or anyone made you believe that it was. There are lots of stories of actors, musicians, entrepreneurs, politicians, writers or artists who have reached the highest pinnacles of their chosen field without having gained a single academic qualification. These are obviously exceptions and I'm not suggesting that this is an excuse not to work hard at school, because whatever you do, communication skills and good literacy and numeracy are always important. However, even if you think you aren't going to get straight grade As in everything, you can still do well. There are many jobs that may not depend solely on academic ability, but proper training and a will to succeed can lead to high levels of achievement. Industries such as catering, textiles, computing and word processing, electrical engineering and design, fine art, music or technical drawing often

Discovering your talents
While you're still at school, try out as many extra activities as you can. You may discover that you have a talent for dancing, acting or making music, which could lead to a career.

look for practical rather than academic abilities. Many caring professions also allow for training while you are working. Your school or college will advise you on the numerous courses and training schemes available that can help you here.

WHEN SCHOOL SEEMS BORING

Some girls find school life irrelevant. They look forward to leaving as soon as they can so they can have the freedom for which they yearn. Not doing well academically may reinforce this desire. They see little reason in investing time and effort in school which they see as constantly interfering with social activities. People and not lessons nearly always come first on their list of priorities. Without incentives or pressures to study, such girls view school work largely as a waste of time. Parents, too, can contribute to these feelings if they don't regard a girl's academic achievements as important.

There are two sure-fire ways of making school less boring: one is to concentrate on a subject you're really good at or that you simply enjoy doing – and there's bound to be one. The other is to attach yourself like a limpet to a teacher who inspires you – there's always one of those around too. If you do, wonderful things will flow from your actions. We learn more about *ourselves*, as well as subjects, when we get close to a project we love. As we discover our hidden talents, our enthusiasms, what turns us on, we may see ourselves in a new light and never be the same again. A really good teacher can light your rocket fuel so that it burns and carries you for years. My Latin teacher was such a person. Latin, you say, how boring. She made it exciting, we remembered her every word, it was fun, it was my favourite lesson. And she taught me how to transform a chore into a joy. A good teacher can do that for you.

UNAUTHORIZED ABSENCE

Some girls absent themselves from school because this is their way of rejecting the monotony and the seemingly stupid rules to which they have to conform there. But it can also be the case that you're pressurized into staying home by one or both of your parents because there's no-one else to do the housework or look after small children while they are at work. If you do start to stay at home, you'll fall behind in your school work and going back will become more and more difficult. Once you drop out, it's an easy step to avoid school and spend your time going out or just staying at home playing music. So if you are getting pressure from your parents, rather than pressure from your own friends, remind your parents that it is actually against the law for them to keep you at home. But if you're staying away from school because you want to, and your parents don't know about it, remember that the school will soon contact your parents and you will be called to account for your absence.

COPING WITH BULLIES

Some girls begin to hate going to school because they are being bullied. Bullying of girls by girls is an unfortunate fact, and is becoming more prevalent. It is often insidious because it takes the form of taunting and ostracization, rather than physical violence – although this too can happen. It sometimes takes place outside the school premises or on the school bus, away from the eyes of vigilant teachers so, even if your school has a strong anti-bullying stance, the problem still arises.

If you're a victim of bullying, don't keep it to yourself. Tell your parents, or let your teachers know in confidence. No-one should have to endure this sort of thing, which can be very destructive to vulnerable young people of either sex, but for girls in particular it can trigger severe psychological problems such as anorexia nervosa. Even if the bullies who are tormenting you swear you to secrecy with threats, the only way the cycle of bullying can be broken is to tell someone in authority so the bullies can be challenged. Bullies are often themselves the victims of bullying, perhaps at home, and need help too to change their behaviour patterns.

Ask your parents to contact the school and have a confidential chat with the teacher in charge of pupils' welfare. If things are really bad, and if the timing fits in with your public examination schedule, you might be able to transfer to another school. If not, it may be better to grit your teeth and stick it out until you've taken your exams at 16, then transfer at this point. Also, school is no longer compulsory after 16 and you can assess the alternative of going out to work.

Improving your self-esteem
Learning a skill, such as judo, can boost your overall self-confidence, making you feel more able to cope with bullies.

AFTER 16 – WHAT THEN?

Like many other girls, I wanted to leave school at 16. I felt a great desire to be independent, to be working and to be earning money of my own. I wanted to stop studying and start enjoying myself. Fortunately for me, my parents and teachers persuaded me to do otherwise. I returned to school after the summer holidays and continued to study for A levels and then went on to medical school. Thank heavens my parents and teachers won me over.

If you are a girl who has academic ability, it would be a great shame if you didn't go on to further study, because it's then that you can really start to enjoy complex and more specialized work. Besides this, your relationships with teachers will become easier, more friendly and more informal, you're given responsibility and you're treated as an adult. Don't forget that because education is no longer compulsory after 16, you have a much wider choice of institution in which to study – you may stay on at your own school, or transfer to a designated sixth form centre or to a further education college, where you may be studying alongside adults.

You should also be very aware that by staying on to do A levels you're possibly preparing for a university career and university life, which will offer independence, living away from home, a new social life and an open academic curriculum. Don't, therefore, be tempted to leave school on a mere whim.

THINKING ABOUT A CAREER

If you know what sort of job or career you want to pursue, you have to get career advice early, and this means usually at around age 14 or 15. Most schools begin careers guidance at this age, and increasingly there are opportunities for useful work experience with local businesses and professionals that is usually organized through the school.

Careers guidance will help you choose the right subjects to study so that a particular career will be open to you. However, beware of closing off any future options by specializing too early. You may change your mind later and it will be too late to go back – although you can take certain extra GCSEs while doing your A levels.

LATE LEARNERS

If you're desperate to leave school at 16, it's probably best to do so, but this need not mean that your interest in learning is over, nor that you will never take up learning again.

Many people are late developers and it's only in their late teens or their early twenties that they have a great yearning to go back to college, night classes or university and continue their education. These "mature" students very often turn out to be the most dedicated students and the highest achievers. So if you find you need this kind of breathing space, take it, provided that you really are doing it for the right reasons. You may find it much easier to learn later on.

However, time spent on your education when you're young is by far and away the best option you can exercise. It's usually a lot harder to find the time, energy and money to go back to studying later on in life.

CAREER OPTIONS

Here's a representative, but by no means exhaustive, list of career options that you might also want to consider:

- *Architectural technician*
- *Chartered surveyor*
- *Car mechanic*
- *Dental assistant*
- *Cartographer*
- *Interior decorator*
- *Dispensing optician*
- *Quantity surveyor*
- *Pharmacy technician*
- *Landscape architect*
- *Meteorological technician*
- *Horticultural engineer*
- *DTP (desk-top publishing) operator*

The aim of most modern education systems is to provide a rounded education for as long as possible and to keep you studying the broadest possible range of subjects. Make sure that your careers officers know what kind of career you want to pursue, so that they can put you in touch with recruitment departments in different professions and industries, and also point you in the direction of the different training or university courses that you should be aiming for.

Keep an open mind One of the most important ways you can help yourself to get an interesting job and have a fruitful career is to keep your mind open. Don't make stereotypical assumptions about the kind of role that you will have as a female in society. Equal opportunities legislation means that all possibilities should be open to you. However, there is still some hidden discrimination, so you may have to be determined if you choose a career in which women workers remain a minority.

Many careers need specialist training at college or university and, given girls' general high levels of achievement up to the age of 16, there really isn't any reason why they shouldn't succeed at this higher level as well. At higher examination levels, boys tend to catch up with girls (probably because they mature later), but girls achieve the same sort of results as boys at this level in most subjects except physics. It's only when they get to university that young men overtake the girls, with fewer young women achieving first class degrees, though this may be more to do with teacher prejudice than with ability. On the other hand, fewer young women fail outright than young men.

What these statistics mean is that you can succeed in any area as well as men when it comes to academic or vocational ability, but at this level you may still have to overcome old-fashioned and ingrained prejudices towards women. The trick is not to let that put you off. If you work hard and achieve good results, you have the right to be treated on equal terms with your fellow students, whether they are boys or girls.

Sources of career information When it's time to think about choosing a career, girls often draw on images found in books and magazines, on television and through observing and talking with the people immediately around them. You may be drawn to one of the caring professions, once thought of as the traditional role for women, but there's no reason why you shouldn't consider being an architect, a lawyer, a builder or a civil engineer (see column, left).

Most newspapers today include special business and careers supplements where you can read interesting background articles on a wide range of industries. There are also large-scale careers fairs in most big cities for you to visit. These, as well as your own school or college careers advisers, can guide you towards career options you may never have thought of and for which you don't necessarily need high academic qualifications; although you'll probably need training, some of which may have to be at a college.

Don't go along to a careers discussion with a blank mind. Make a list of all the areas you're interested in and ones in which you have particular skills. Don't forget the armed services, which offer good careers, sound training, and in most cases, enable you to serve alongside men in equal positions. At the end of four or seven years, you could find yourself highly qualified and very much in demand in a public service job or in the business world.

Research
Finding out about what you want to do is very important and books and magazines can be good sources of useful, up-to-date information.

OVERCOMING PREJUDICE

Don't take any notice if anyone says these kinds of things to you:

- *It's a man's job.*

- *You'd look silly in a pair of dirty overalls under a car.*

- *Girls aren't interested in engineering.*

- *You don't hear of many female executives.*

- *Girls don't become pilots.*

- *Girls don't do technical drawing.*

- *It's not right for a girl to do the same work as a boy.*

- *You don't have girl lorry drivers because usually the stuff inside the lorry is too heavy for a girl to lift.*

- *It's unladylike.*

- *Boys are able to put up with things that girls can't.*

- *I think this job would be too complicated for a girl.*

- *Girls don't have to earn quite as much as a boy as he will soon have to support a family. Boys need the steady, well-paid jobs if they are going to get married.*

WHAT GOES INTO A CV

Your CV should include the following in this order:

• *Your name, address and telephone number.*

• *Your date of birth and age.*

• *The name, address and dates of schools and colleges attended.*

• *Qualifications – subject examinations with grades, and dates taken; plus any other certificates such as music, drama, sport, youth awards.*

• *If you're looking for a short-term position for a few months before taking up a college or university place, give details of the course you're going to study, and where you'll be studying, as well as the start date, so that your employer knows exactly how long you're going to be available for work.*

• *Previous temporary employment, such as weekend, evening or holiday work, with dates and names of employers.*

• *Voluntary work, including any community work, fund-raising, or amateur arts involvement, such as membership of a drama group or amateur orchestra.*

• *All your interests – don't leave any out. Even playing computer games can count because it shows that you're familiar with computers and probably have quick reflexes.*

• *Future training or education plans. If you're taking a year off before going to university, explain this.*

THE WORLD OF WORK

If you decide to look for a job, rather than going on to further education or university, get as much help as you can on how to apply for jobs and handle interviews. Some schools may have careers departments which will set up dummy interviews, often with professionals or local business people, to help you with the technique. They should also show you how to write good application letters and fill in application forms. Putting together a lively Curriculum Vitae – literally a life history – is an important part of this.

Writing your CV   Prepare a draft CV on a word processor, if possible, before you even need to think about applying for jobs, and then all you have to do is adapt it to suit your prospective employer.

Obviously, you're not going to have much of a record of employment, although holiday or weekend work is relevant because it shows that you've got some experience of workplace routines. Give the names of two people as references. Most employers ask for this anyway, but line them up beforehand. They need to be people in responsible positions who know you, such as teachers, youth workers, church leaders or past employers. You should ask their permission first, and let them know that they may be contacted by potential employers.

Going to interviews   It's exciting but nerve-racking to go to your first job interview, but you can feel confident by following a few simple rules. (These apply equally to going for an interview for a college or university place.)

• When you get invited for an interview, write as soon as possible to confirm that you can be there on the day and at the time requested. If it's difficult, be open about it, and ask for another appointment. Employers and universities realize that people may have commitments.

• Find out as much as you can about the company (or university) beforehand so that you can tailor your answers. Almost all interviewers will ask why you want to join their particular organization rather than any other.

• Go to bed early the night before, and work out what you're going to wear in advance so that you're not in a flap in the morning. Aim to look smart, but not flashy.

• Work out how to get to the interview location in time, and leave plenty of time so that you're not late – this gives a bad impression from the start. However, in case you're let down by public transport, make sure you've got the contact telephone number so you can let them know.

• Don't worry about being on edge, the interviewer will be expecting it and a good one will try to put you at your ease. Sit down when you're asked. Always refer to "Mr X" or "Miss Y" unless you're invited to use first names.

• When you answer questions, don't just answer "yes" or "no". Enlarge on what you're asked. Speak clearly and look the interviewer in the eye. Don't forget to smile.

• Don't be afraid to ask questions – most interviewers will ask you if there is anything you want to know, usually towards the end of the interview. If it hasn't been made clear or you're not sure, ask the interviewer to confirm the salary, and whether you'll be expected to work overtime or weekends, and about holidays.

• You may be offered the job (or place) straightaway. If you're undecided, ask for time to think about it, even if it's just overnight. Go home and discuss it with your parents or teachers so that you can decide calmly.

STAYING AT HOME OR MOVING OUT

In a way, it's easier to stay on at school or college than to leave and get a job. There are fewer upheavals. If they can afford to, your parents will almost certainly continue to support you both financially and emotionally in your period of further study. But if you do want or have to leave school to take a job, you're going to have to be responsible for many new aspects of your life, including organizing yourself, and making sure that your clothes are clean and ironed each morning. You have to start working out your spending, budgeting for lunches, deciding what to spend your money on, whether you are going to save and how much you are going to contribute to your parents for your upkeep.

Most young people need the comfort, company and support of a family to take on all these new challenges; you will probably find it much too hard and worrying to leave school and home at the same time. You're probably not ready or able to cope with such enormous changes in your life, so if circumstances permit, leave school and take up your new job while you're still living at home.

Useful Addresses

If you would like to receive information from any of the addresses listed below, please send a stamped, addressed envelope with your enquiry.

General

Citizens Advice Bureau (CAB)
Middleton House
115-123 Pentonville Road
London N1 9LZ
Tel: 0171 833 2181

Driving Instructors' Association
Safety House
Beddington Farm Road
Croydon
Surrey CR0 4ZX
Tel: 0181 665 5151

Eating Disorders Association
First Floor, Wensum House
103 Prince of Wales Road
Norwich NR1 1DW
Tel: 01603 621414

Health Education Authority (HEA)
Trevelyan House
30 Great Peter Street
London SW1P 2HW
Tel: 0171 222 5300

National Association for Pre-menstrual Syndrome
PO Box 72
Sevenoaks
Kent TN13 1XQ
Tel: 01732 741709

Pregnancy and Contraception

British Pregnancy Advisory Service (BPAS)
Austy Manor, Wootton Wawen
Solihull, West Midlands B95 6BX
Tel: 0121 643 1461

A national network of clinics offering counselling, pregnancy testing and abortions

Brook Advisory Centre
233 Tottenham Court Road
London W1P 9AE
Tel: 0171 580 2991

Provides advice for young people (under 26) on personal relationships, contraception, abortion and pregnancy tests

Family Planning Association (FPA)
2–12, Pentonville Road
London N1 9FP
Tel: 0171 837 5432

Pregnancy Advisory Service (PAS)
11–13 Charlotte Street
London W1P 1HD
Tel: 0171 637 8962

Counselling

Childline
Freepost 1111
London N1 0BR
Freephone: 0800 1111

Cruse Bereavement Care
Helpline: 0181 332 7227

Gay and Lesbian Switchboard
Tel: 0171 837 7324
(24-hour)

London Lesbian Line
Helpline: 0171 251 6911

National Aids Helpline
Tel: 0800 567123

Rape Crisis Centre
Helpline: 0171 837 1600

The Samaritans
Tel: 0345 909090

Look in your phone book for the local number

Sexual Health

Herpes Association Helpline
Tel: 0171 609 9061

Positively Women
347–349 City Road
London EC1V 1LR
Helpline: 0171 713 0222
All other enquiries:
0171 713 0444

Counselling for HIV-positive women

Terence Higgins Trust
52-54 Grays Inn Road
London WC1X 8JU
Tel: 0171 242 1010

HIV and AIDS helpline

Drugs and Alcohol

Action on Smoking and Health (ASH)
16 Fitzhardinge Street
London W1H 9PL
Tel: 0171 224 0743

Drinkline
Tel: 0345 320202

Drugs in Schools Helpline
Call Release helpline on
0345 366666 for a referral

Information service for parents, pupils and teachers

National Drugs Helpline
Tel: 0800 776600

Free 24-hour counselling service – calls will not appear on itemized bills

Turning Point
London office:
Tel: 0171 702 2300

Scotland office:
Tel: 0141 418 0882

Drugs counselling service

INDEX

ACKNOWLEDGMENTS

Dorling Kindersley would like to thank the following individuals and organizations for their contribution to this book:

PHOTOGRAPHY
All photography by Hanya Chlaha,
Andy Crawford, John Garrett, Steve Gorton,
Dave King, Ray Moller, Paul Vennins

ADDITIONAL EDITORIAL ASSISTANCE
Nicky Adamson, Dawn Bates, Claire Cross,
David Summers

DTP ASSISTANCE
Rajen Shah

INDEX
Hilary Bird

TEXT FILM
The Brightside Partnership, London